ROSE CITY AUDITION

ROSE CITY AUDITION

**Stories from
My Portland Adventure**

M. J. Coreil

Tropic of Candor Publications

Lafayette, Louisiana

Copyright © 2019 M. J. Coreil

All rights reserved. No part of this publication may be reproduced or transmitted in any form or by any means, electronic or mechanical, including photocopying, recording or any other information storage and retrieval system, without the written permission of the author, except for brief quotations in a review.

Paperback ISBN: 978-1-7341145-0-8
Epub ISBN: 978-1-7341145-1-5

Tropic of Candor Publications
Lafayette, Louisiana
www.tropicofcandor.com
mjcoreil@tropicofcandor.com

Cover and book interior design by Megan Barra
Cover and interior photographs by M. J. Coreil

Names and biographical details of individuals have been changed.

Four of the essays in this book were originally published in a slightly different form in the following sources.

"Soul Repair," Oregon Humanities, Spring 2015, 40, https://www.oregonhumanities.org/rll/magazine/fix-spring-2015/posts5/.

"Smile Your Way to Success," The Satirist, December 4, 2015, https://www.thesatirist.com/satires/smile_your_way_to_success.html.

"Snuggling with Peers," originally published as "Cuddle Parties: Would You Snuggle with Strangers?" Single at Heart (blog), PsycCentral, February 2, 2017, https://blogs.psychcentral.com/single-at heart/2017/01/snuggle-parties-would-you-cuddle-with-strangers-guest-post-by-m-j-coreil/.

"Somewhere on the Spectrum," Ursa Minor: UC Berkeley Extension's Art & Literature Review 2 (2017):70-75.

Contents

Acknowlegements *ix*
Prologue *xi*
Portland—Paragon or Chimera? 1
Soul Repair 23
The Specter of Michael Hewitt 27
Snuggling with Peers 41
The Oregon Country Fair 57
Docent Corps Takes Portland 65
Smile Your Way to Success 73
Mindful Meddling 77
The Springwater Corridor 81
Good Hair Day 91
Chickenmania 97
A Reluctant Rosarian 121
Sesame Salmon Baked in Foil 131
Two Minutes of Totality 135
Building Community 151
Somewhere on the Spectrum 171
Finding Home 185
Epilogue 201
Notes 206
About the Author 207

ROSE CITY AUDITION

Acknowledgements

The honest feedback of many readers helped shepherd me away from the academic writing style I'd honed over decades. That transition is still in progress, but I especially appreciate the guidance from my two writing groups in Portland. For encouragement, support, and advice, I'm grateful to Graham Coreil-Allen and Susan Perez. Several reviewers weighed in helpfully on all or parts of the manuscript: Mary Phillips, Ariel Lewiton, Summer Grace, Kristin Houlihan, Chris Haight, Paul Coreil, Arlene Coreil, Armand Coreil, Sid Kere, Robin Leigh, Ed Gauthier, Carol Rice, and Sue Schleifer. Luke Coreil kindly retrieved a photo from the family album. My talented book designer, Megan Barra, was a pleasure to work with, and Libby Nehrbass provided valuable editing. Lastly, I'm thankful to Elliot Coreil-Allen for unconditional kindness and acceptance.

ROSE CITY AUDITION

Prologue

Late nineteenth century visitors to Portland, noting that roses thrived in the warm, moist climate of the Willamette Valley, bestowed the title "City of Roses" on the bustling new city. The name stuck. The Portland Rose Society was established in 1889. Thousands of rose bushes were planted along twenty miles of streets for the Lewis and Clark Centennial Exposition of 1905. Two years later, the inaugural Rose Festival began a tradition that remains the most important civic event of the year, celebrated with parades, concerts, art events, navy ships, rose displays, and a royal court. The International Rose Test Garden, established in 1917, today counts over eight thousand varietals.

Like its namesake, I wanted to thrive in the Rose City, set down roots in its fertile soil, absorb its heady atmosphere, and produce blooms of vivid color. I sought to experience the wonders of the city's festival ambience, eccentricities, alternative lifestyles, and progressive values. I tried my best to become an authentic Portlander. Along the way I wrote essays to capture my experience. These stories reveal a garden of delights, disappointments, and reflections on what it means to belong somewhere.

ROSE CITY AUDITION

Portland—Paragon or Chimera?

Most people move across country for work, love, or family. Sometimes they move for adventure, as I did, but earlier in life, not at sixty-one, single, and without connections. In Portland, I started from scratch.

My adulation of Portland, Oregon, dated back to the early 1970s when I read an article in Utne Reader about the city's innovative local currency called "greenbucks." The system aimed to support the local economy by encouraging people to spend their money close to home, epitomizing, in my mind, Portland's progressive worldview and cutting-edge leadership in creating sustainable communities.

Forty years later, after finding my way to Portland, I wrote to the editor of Utne Reader, hoping to get my hands on a copy of that fateful article. He checked the archives but found nothing on the topic. Moreover, he said the magazine didn't begin publication until 1984, so if I saw such an article in the 1970s, it appeared in another source.

What? My recollection was wrong? Where in the hell could I have read about a local currency?

I researched community currencies and learned about several experiments in American cities, but Portland wasn't mentioned. Neither the Oregon Historical Society nor The Oregonian could find records in their archives of Portland ever having its own currency. In desperation, I interviewed all the native-born locals I knew and even contacted officials and amateur historians. No one had ever heard of greenbucks.

Eventually, I accepted the fact that my inspiration story was illusory. Could my idealized image of the city be chimerical as well? This planted a seed of doubt about everything I'd always believed about Portland, but I refused to let a memory glitch taint my love affair with the Rose City, which had become a paragon of sensible growth, environmental stewardship, mass transit, sustainable development, and community involvement.

Why Did I Move to Portland?

I'd been asked this question more often than any other since arriving in Portland. My answers were fourfold. First, I'd always admired Portland as one of the most progressive, interesting cities in the country, and I'd hoped to live there someday. After retiring from my university job, I realized I could live anywhere I chose! Second, I'd lived my entire life in the US Southeast and wanted to experience a different part of the country. Unprompted, a Florida neighbor once told me my "earthiness" reminded her of someone who might live in Oregon. Third, I'd grown up in Louisiana and lived in Kentucky, Texas, and Florida. Everywhere I'd lived, my liberal views were shared by only a minority of the people around me. For once, I wanted to fit in with the majority, to live in a blue-green state where people exhorted openly and loudly their progressive ideas. Even my Tampa psychotherapist, who said she normally didn't advise people to make a geographic move to find greater happiness, encouraged me to relocate. Fourth, my younger son, Elliot, had moved to Seattle, and my older son, Graham, lived in Baltimore. Given a choice of East or West Coast to be near one of them, the Pacific Northwest held greater appeal.

Over the years, whenever I heard someone mention Portland, my attention heightened. What glimpse of the city might I get? If I met someone who actually lived in Portland, I envisioned them imbued with good fortune and looked eagerly for clues to life in their everyday world. I incorporated these impressions into fantasies about living in a utopian community.

The Long Quest to Live in the Promised Land

My quest to move to Portland began around 2000, when Graham graduated from high school, and I realized if I wanted to make another move in my professional life, I should do it soon. I'd been teaching for twenty years and planned to continue for at least another ten. I made contacts at Portland State University and expressed interest in future positions.

In 2004 I landed a job interview as Director of PSU's School of Community Health. The position was similar to the one I held at the time, chair of the Department of Community and Family Health at the University of South Florida in Tampa. I prepared meticulously for an opportunity of a lifetime.

Like so much of my fieldwork as an anthropologist, my relationship to Portland combined spectacular highs with painful lows.

In her seventieth decade, my mother developed abdominal pain of mysterious origin. Exploratory surgery was needed to narrow down the possibilities. During the operation, my mother went into respiratory distress and had to be put on a ventilator. I visited her in early May 2004, while she could only communicate by facial expression and gestures.

Mom died ten days before my PSU interview. Her loss sucked all the energy out of me and my five brothers. It landed my father in the intensive care unit; he would die ten days after my interview.

Over the three days I spent meeting with administrators, faculty, and students, I stayed in constant contact with my brothers, prepared to fly home at a moment's notice. Going through the motions of the interview in a daze, I recall having difficulty making conversation. Moreover, I knew I didn't fit into the college's business-oriented culture, but I'd have accepted that strain just to live in Portland, where even watching the streetcar pull up to the stop on the PSU campus gave me a thrill.

Now I understand why the perfectly suited administrator in the well-appointed office looked at me blankly when I told him my inspiration story about greenbucks. At the time, I assumed he had mentally demoted me to a countercultural dweeb foolish enough to consider local currencies worthwhile. In truth, he didn't know what I was talking about. Needless to say, I didn't get the job.

Six years later, when the university offered early retirement to tenured faculty, I grabbed it. Soon after, my son moved to Seattle and I joined a creative writing group in Tampa.

I'd been looking into house swapping sites for Portland, thinking I could spend short periods there as a visitor. When the idea occurred to simply relocate longer-term, I knew instantly I'd do it. I'd rent out my Tampa house and live in Portland for a year or more.

For once, being single and unfettered by the need to negotiate a big decision with a partner clearly benefitted me. I'd felt the deprivation of the single life long enough. Time to celebrate its advantages.

Becoming a Real Portlander

With my life's possessions pared down to two packing cubes, I arrived in Portland on October 2, 2012. The excitement I felt reminded me of going to a county fair, where exotic booths, fascinating exhibits, scary rides, educational displays, and a cornucopia of food beckoned the patron.

I felt internal pressure to maximize my experience of the lifestyle, events, and opportunities offered by Portland and Oregon. Now was my chance, and I'd better make the most of it. I vowed to sample the city's bounty, relish its quirks, immerse myself in intentional communities, and cultivate an insider's appreciation for what it's really like to live there. I approached my mission like an autoethnography, using my personal experiences to understand the Portland milieu as one might study another culture.

I'd told my son Elliot I wanted to find hippies in Portland. Instead, I found hipsters. Young, college-educated transplants, some apparently living on trust funds because they didn't seem to have jobs. Looking for the good life, like me. I knew my age and temperament disqualified me from any claims to hipness, so I cultivated groups compatible with my conventional background.

Portland is home to every conceivable interest group. There are hundreds of Meetups, the ever-popular networking venue for new arrivals and the chronically gregarious, some so specialized you'd think they'd have only five members—the Trans Millennials of Scandinavian Descent Alpine Hiking Meetup, for example (I'm joking). During my sojourn, I belonged to a dozen: Oregon Touch; Feisty Women Over Fifty-Five; Social Singles 60+; Cinema Paradiso; Netflix Film Club; Foodie!; Petanque Club; Write to Publish; Nonfiction Writers of Portland; Portland French Connection; Laughter Yoga; Fishing 101.

These groups were great for meeting people, finding fun activities, learning about the city, and inspiring me to write satires. Yet, after five years, I belonged to only one Meetup—Write to Publish—where I workshopped this book. The other groups fell by the wayside one by one as I lost interest in continually meeting new people and going through introductions and small talk. I yearned for a genuine sense of community, a feeling of belonging, and the security of being able to count on others to care about me. After five years, I'd burned out, discouraged about creating community, opting to limit my social engagement to the meditation center I joined in 2016.

In Portland, for the first time in my adult life, I had the freedom to do as much volunteer work as I pleased. I became a receptionist/tour guide and developed an ethnobotany tour for Leach Botanical Garden. I trained to become a Master Recycler and stood at tables to answer questions. I lugged my old Singer sewing machine to Repair Cafes to mend garments. I checked tools in and out of the Southeast Portland Tool Library. I inspected newly planted saplings for Friends of Trees.

My volunteer work was profiled in Resourceful PDX, the newsletter for sustainable living sponsored by Portland's Bureau of Planning and Sustainability. The lead article in the June 2016 issue included a close-up of me sewing. Graham said the city had recognized me as a model citizen. I badly needed the boost. Recovering from a devastating failure at chicken raising, my Portlander credentials needed affirmation.

Exploring Oregon

From the start, I tried to balance my exploration of Portland with getting to know the rest of the state. With the zeal of an ethnographer, I mapped out the terrain for discovery. My first goal was to visit each of the Seven Wonders of Oregon. I had visited Mt. Hood in 2002, when I attended a conference in Portland, so I had six wonders left: the Columbia River Gorge, the Oregon Coast, Crater Lake, the Painted Hills, Smith Rock, and the Wallowas.

Of all the wonders, I loved the Painted Hills best, with Crater Lake a close second. The coast is magnificent and stunning, but I missed the warm waters, gentle breezes, and powdery white beaches of the Gulf of Mexico, near which I'd lived most of my life.

Interspersed with my visits to the seven wonders, I took in Astoria, Fort Clatsop, Aurora, the Scandinavian Midsummer Festival, the Pendleton Roundup, the Sisters Outdoor Quilt Show, Breitenbush, Hells Canyon, Champoeg State Heritage Area, the Oregon Garden, Silver Falls, Kam Wah Chung State Heritage Site, the Malheur Wildlife Refuge, and The Oregon Country Fair, just to name a few.

Within the city itself, I methodically visited parks, nature preserves, and hiking trails. I sampled dozens of restaurants and pubs. I attended music and dance concerts, plays, lectures, and art exhibits. I rallied with Black Lives Matter and joined the Resistance after the 2016 election. I showed up for pride events and joined Basic Rights Oregon. I mingled with the crowds at outdoor festivals and signed up for neighborhood walking tours. I indulged my soccer enthusiasm at Timbers and Thorns matches. I took classes in hula, Nia movement, yoga, Jazzercise, and ecstatic dance. Twice I witnessed the dramatic swirling of Vaux's swifts into Chapman School. During the holidays, I took in the light shows at the Grotto, Peacock Lane, and the racetrack.

Concurrent with my explorations, I made extensive repairs to my fixer-upper home. Over two years I hired contractors to do major work on the yard, siding, walls, floors, windows, and gutters. I renovated the upstairs into a cozy snuggle space. The strain of these repairs, coupled with the drive to experience everything in town, would snap over chicken raising and plunge me into a mental health crisis. To cope, I began meditating and joined a spiritual community. To my amazement, I became a Buddhist practitioner.

Making Friends

Starting from scratch to make friends in a new city is tough. Elliot, in his late twenties, experienced this in Seattle, and I, in my early sixties, did so in Portland. Everyone says that's just the way things are these days in big cities. In Seattle, they call it the "Seattle Freeze." In Portland, the city's reputation for greeting newcomers with politeness but not true friendliness is dubbed the "Portland Politesse." A friend's twenty-something son had moved to Portland a few years prior, but never felt at home there and soon left. As an older single woman, I knew making social connections wouldn't be easy.

From the beginning, I recognized that the biggest challenge would be my autistic tendencies. My mild disability isn't obvious to people when they first get to know me. They might note my intense forthrightness and over time become increasingly uncomfortable with my direct interactional style. But my atypical pattern of autism, probably linked to congenital rubella, rarely garners empathy in social situations, even after I've disclosed my condition and asked for understanding. Instead, I often offend people and experience social distancing. This interpersonal liability hovered in my awareness as I navigated unfamiliar territory. I'm certain it played no small part in my struggle to find community and cultivate friendships.

I'd hoped to make friends with both men and women my age. The men I met didn't seem interested in just being friends. They quickly found girlfriends then spent all their time with their sweethearts. My friendships with women were complicated and often strained. Of the six women I befriended (defined as getting together more than once individually) over five years, only one remained a friend when I left. The other friendships worked well for one or two years but ended with our first disagreement. In each case, one or the other of us wasn't committed enough to work through our differences. In later life, people seem to be set in their ways and resist compromise.

None of the women I met who were near my age had moved to Portland for its lifestyle, as I had. If they hadn't always lived in Oregon, or moved there for work, the women likely relocated to be near a daughter or, less often, a son. Three of my female friends and many women I met had moved for that reason. Some had grandchildren in the area as well. In addition to their families, most women had dense social networks of friends and colleagues, especially if they'd lived there a long time. These well-connected women didn't seem to have a lot of room for new friends.

In her book about women's friendships, *You're the Only One I Can Tell*, Deborah Tannen notes this challenge for older single women who seek to make friends after moving to a new city to be near children or to enjoy a better climate. As one woman explained to her, the "people you meet already have friends—and busy lives. They're not looking for new ones. Even if you do make friends, they know so little about who you are. You can't exactly catch them up on your whole life".[1] More than any other factor, the difficulty I encountered in making friends and finding community weighed heavily in my eventual decision to leave the city.

At times, I envied my closest friend in Portland, Martha, whom I met through a mutual acquaintance. Martha had moved there to be near one daughter, spent extended periods with another daughter in Texas, hosted a relative twice a year for long stays, and often visited a best friend from childhood in Eugene. The two of us couldn't be more different in our approach to settling in Portland. While I avidly sought new connections with individuals and groups, Martha seemed content with the social life she brought with her. She moved to Portland a year before I did, and as far as I knew, she'd made no new friends, apart from me and the one I introduced to her, nor had she joined any groups. She didn't need to. Her life was already full.

While I couldn't count many close friends in my adopted city, I made many casual friends and accumulated a diverse contact list of dozens of Portland phone numbers. In 2015 I threw a Mardi Gras party for a houseful of guests from my volunteer work, snuggle parties, social groups, and exercise class. No neighbors were invited because, to my surprise, people on my street didn't socialize. In four years on my block, I'd never been invited into the home of any neighbor, despite having friendly sidewalk conversations, and I wasn't aware of any neighbors who visited one another either. I invited the woman across the street over for coffee, but she never reciprocated. My gut feeling was people preferred to maintain a polite distance from neighbors, so I accepted this norm.

My Neighborhoods

Portland's distinctive, walkable neighborhoods are often cited as one of the key features of the city's desirability as a place to live. Most close-in neighborhoods looked like miniature towns, with a main street, shops, eateries, and a single-screen movie theater. One's address became a key aspect of identity—the closer in, the more prestigious.

I spent my first week in Portland in an upscale rental in the historic Alphabet District, treating myself to a taste of the trendy life (only steps from celebrity chef Paley's Place!), followed by three weeks in a modest studio off Hawthorne, the hip neighborhood where I hoped to settle. Luckily, I could walk most places, because I feared crashing my car into one of the aggressive cyclists who zoomed everywhere.

The Hawthorne neighborhood appeared every bit as hip as reputed, although somewhat shabbier than I'd imagined. But finding an apartment there proved challenging, since few vacancies could be found in the month of October (I'd been duly warned). Available flats were either incredibly tiny or too expensive. I set my sights farther east, where affordable rentals were more abundant. In Hazelwood, I found a lovely, bright, split-level duplex on a quiet, tree-lined street near 119th Avenue, a few blocks south of Burnside. Little did I know I had chosen to live in what many Portlanders considered the boonies, and I'd have to overcome residential prejudice to find acceptance.

The first inkling my address might be a handicap came at a Meetup gathering. At these events, as in most encounters around town, the essential biographical facts had to be established: *Are you a native or a transplant? How long have you lived in Portland? Where do you live?* Yikes—three strikes and you're an outcast!

I soon learned people consider the "outer east side" decidedly uncool, its residents the object of sympathy or indifference. The most common response was a blank stare. For some, the outer limits began east of 82nd, for others, anything past 60th, and for the purists, beyond 39th. One interlocutor dismissed everything east of 92nd as part of Gresham, the next town, his tone implying "that boring suburb," although technically Portland extended as far as 175th.

After the stark reality of zip code snobbery sunk in, I began fudging where I lived. The ambiguous "on the east side" or "in the southeast" sounded much better than "near 122nd."

Sometimes I headed off social dismissal by joking, "I hope you won't hold it against me." Other times, I praised the joys of having both a sunny back deck and a shady front porch, covered parking, a library and community center within walking distance, plenty retail stores, and a MAX stop six blocks away. If this elicited a glimmer of interest, I waxed eloquent on the majestic firs outside my window, the colorful plum trees gracing the sidewalks, and the green oasis of Ventura Park. I *did not* mention that there wasn't a single coffee shop within miles, unless, of course, you count Village Inn and Denny's.

During the first few weeks living close-in, I had marveled at the lack of diversity in the people around me. Are there only white people living in Portland, I'd wondered? The census showed about a quarter of the population was nonwhite, so people of color had to live somewhere. In the far east, I found them in my culturally diverse neighborhood, where African American, Hispanic, Asian, and Eastern European residents were commonplace. After living in Florida for twenty-five years, seeing people of other ethnicities felt normal. The small eateries and businesses tailored to this mix imparted a pleasing flavor to our community.

Walking around Hazelwood I found delights and surprises. Billboards in Russian, a plethora of Mexican restaurants and carts, ubiquitous strip clubs and medical marijuana dispensaries (that guidebook was right!), impromptu soccer games on vacant lots, neighbors that stopped to chat. Nearby Leach Botanical Garden offered wondrous natural delights, and the Springwater Corridor became my favorite sunny hiking trail. However, I was taken aback to find unpaved, deeply rutted streets, at first assuming this reflected hinterland neglect. Later, I discovered dirt streets all over town, something I'd not seen since growing up in rural Louisiana.

After I'd lived in Portland for nine months, I realized I wanted to stay more than a year. In fact, I wanted to buy a house and settle down for a spell. I checked websites that advised people about investing in real estate. For the Portland area, the advice said one should expect to live in a house for at least five years to make the investment worthwhile. No problem there, I thought. I planned to live in the Rose City five to ten years, or until I became feeble and needed more care.

Deciding where to look for a house posed a

dilemma. I was torn between wanting a more desirable neighborhood (not to mention less driving) and resisting social pressure to conform. So what if others viewed the far east as uninteresting, what did I care? Most of the people I met through Meetups lived closer in, their neighborhoods highly "walkable," but I rarely frequented coffee shops, so maybe that didn't matter so much. After all, the longer I lived in Portland, my newbie scores would decline steadily, offsetting an unfashionable street address. If I stayed long enough, Hazelwood would surely take its turn in the spotlight of trendy Portland neighborhoods.

I landed in Sellwood, where I bought a house and lived for four and a half years. This southernmost section of the inner southeast had just begun to change rapidly. Historically a working-class neighborhood with the feel of a small town, Sellwood was transforming into a trendy, family-oriented community with infill development popping up everywhere. I began calling the area Stroller City because of all the toddlers being pushed and pedaled around its shady streets. Someone told me our zip code, 97202, was the top destination for Silicon Valley families relocating from the Bay Area. Increasingly, coffee shops, restaurants, and other businesses had created play areas for the children of their patrons. People without children grumbled about the influx of families and the vibe that created. Healthy and wholesome instead of edgy and hip.

I could live with wholesomeness; it felt safe. But the destruction of older homes to make room for McMansions obscenely out of scale for the neighborhood sparked my ire. My house sat in a row of three made by the same builder in 1952. Barely a year after I moved in, the corner house was demolished, and in its place, two three-story monstrosities were erected so close together only a few feet separated them. The top floor windows overlooked my backyard, which previously had privacy. Four mature conifers were cut down to make room for these 4500-square-foot homes. The one tree left standing, a stinky ailanthus, produced nuisance saplings all over the block.

While Sellwood used to be the go-to neighborhood for antiques, only a few antique stores remained open, most having closed during the 2008 recession. In their place a plethora of gourmet coffee shops had appeared, along with the fashionable artisanal boutiques so scathingly lampooned in the television series *Portlandia*. My favorite was the Portland Homestead Supply, which sold live chickens and goat accessories, canning ware, handmade brooms, and every conceivable tool for fashioning home goods. There were stores dedicated to socks, crafts, games, medicinal herbs, and handcrafted knives. Shortly before I moved away, a boutique for specialty butters, both sweet and savory, opened near the movie theater. Gazing in amazement at the selection of flavored butters, I asked myself, *Do we really need a butter shop?* Apparently locals thought we did, because the store seemed to be thriving.

By design of city planners, the densification of housing was happening all over Portland. Multistory apartment complexes began popping up all over town. Several were built in Sellwood after the opening of the light rail line south to Milwaukie. Concerned citizens had little recourse but to push for longer public review periods and to take a stand when exceptionally old or rare trees were slated for removal. They rarely won.

My Name

After I moved to Portland, I changed my name. Twice. First, on the spur of the moment. Again, after much deliberation. I came to view this new identity as emblematic of my nuanced relationship with my adopted city.

Until my senior year of high school, when I had to submit a copy of my birth certificate for a college application, I thought my name was Jeannine Marie Coreil and my birthday was September 27. What a shock to discover that my birth certificate had my given names reversed and my date of birth as September 26. "That's wrong," my mother insisted, "they made a mistake." She dug out my baptismal certificate, pointed and said, "See? Jeannine Marie Coreil, born September 27."

How could hospital personnel have made not one, but two significant mistakes on such an important document? And no one noticed the discrepancy for eighteen years? I could understand getting names reversed, but the wrong date? I wasn't born close to midnight, either, where the day might be confused. Since that discovery I've had to use the new name and date on official documents, and I take the liberty of celebrating a two-day birthday each year.

In my professional life I continued to use the name Jeannine Coreil and had no problems for business transactions and air travel until the security crackdown after 9/11. After that event, names on tickets and other official forms had to match one's identification exactly.

Marie became an alter ego for me. Before moving to Portland, I had used the name as an alias on occasion and in situations where I didn't want to disclose my real name. For example, I often used it in online dating. I also used it with medical providers because my insurance had to be billed correctly.

My decision to become Marie Coreil in my volunteer work in Portland occurred near the end of training to be a Master Recycler. The instructor circulated a list of the names to appear on our official badges and gave us the opportunity to make corrections. I swiftly made the calculus that using the name Marie in public affairs would work best because people in Portland seemed to have difficulty understanding the French pronunciation of Jeannine (a legacy of my Cajun background), much less saying it. It's pronounced "zhah-neen," like the name Jacques. I often had to repeat the name for people, spell it, or give a more American pronunciation, as in Judge Jeanine. I'd rather be called Marie than "djaneen."

The more deliberate name change came when I decided to distinguish my creative writing from my previous work as a medical anthropologist. That's when I adopted the name M. J. Coreil.

Having people address me by a different name than I was used to added to the feeling that, in Portland, I inhabited a different world. Would I become a different person? Would I feel at home in this city? Would the reality of this long-admired community approximate the imagined ideal?

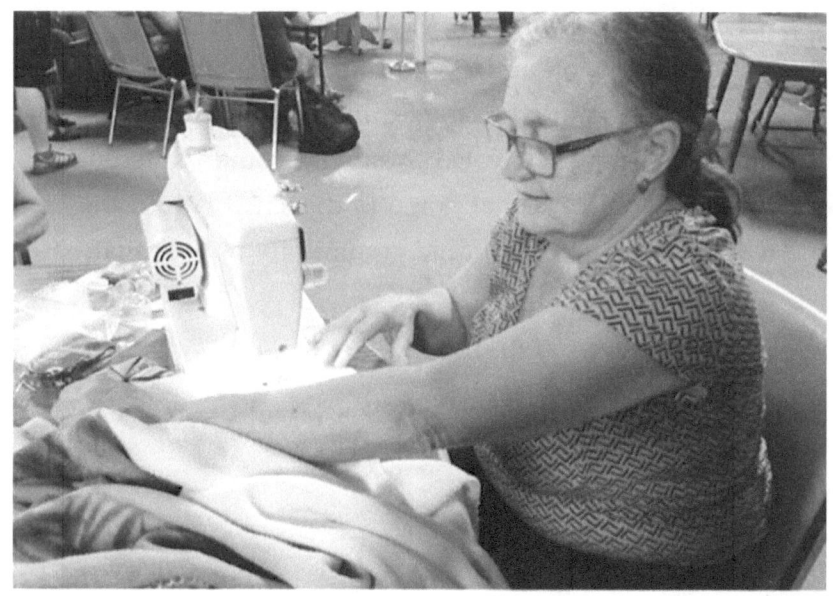

Soul Repair

The faded cotton robe is old and frayed, so threadbare it can scarcely hold a patch. I carefully pin the fabric, hoping it won't tear when I sew the pieces together. It holds. The old man smiles gratefully; I let out a sigh of relief. Around me the metallic rumble of four sewing machines provides the sound track as I take a sip of water and pick up the next item.

Thirty years of cerebral toil in the academic trenches leaves me thought-weary and craving the use of my hands for craft, not for pecking out words. I am volunteering at a repair event, where people bring broken items to be fixed by a team of skilled workers. Once a month we set up shop in donated venues, grouped by task—small appliances, bicycles, jewelry, garments, blade sharpening. The skills I bring are modest at best. Yet I find enormous satisfaction in mending clothes. I feel competent, in command, even hip.

Never mind that my old Singer portable rattles like a jalopy; it works fine for hemming, stitching, patching. Around the spacious room, a volunteer takes apart a toaster, another sharpens scissors on a small sanding belt; elsewhere, a new clasp makes a necklace whole, while a broken bike is hoisted onto a stand. *Let no object enter a landfill that can be saved.*

I smile earnestly at a new customer, a young woman in a hurry. "My parking meter runs out soon so please be quick," she says. Of course she would hand me a zipper to fix, one of the most complicated tasks that many workers refuse to accept. I take my time to do it right, and the client becomes agitated. I don't react because I have entered that so-sweet, serene sewing zone. The woman makes it out the door just in time, repaired dress in bag. I sigh even louder this time, and gulp down more water.

By the end of my three-hour shift, I have repaired six garments. I am tired and weary but feel incredibly accomplished. After-visions of seams coming together, threading needles, hand stitching, edges trimmed, all blur together in a soothing balm. The background din recedes. I can relax because I have done enough.

ROSE CITY AUDITION

The Specter of Michael Hewitt

A knock on the front door at 7:45 on a Saturday night startles me. When I see the police uniform, I think perhaps the officer is going door to door with an advisory. That had happened to me in Tampa, when the cops suspected a fugitive might be hiding in our neighborhood.

"Does Michael Hewitt live here?" the officer asks.

The question takes me by surprise because Hewitt, the previous owner of the house, had passed away more than a year before. I figure this has something to do with Michael's unpaid bills, for which creditors and collection agencies regularly sent letters.

"No, officer, he's deceased," I reply. "I bought the house from his executor."

Officer Wilson relays the information on his radio, then explains that a car had been stopped in downtown Portland and the driver claimed he bought the vehicle from Hewitt a week before. "Not possible," I say, "he's long dead."

The officer thanks me and leaves. A few minutes later, he returns, and my heart begins to pound.

Wilson apologizes for having to disturb me again.

"The driver of the car insists he bought the vehicle out of Michael's driveway, and gave this address. You know nothing about a car sale or anything like that?" he asks.

"No, nothing," I reply.

Wilson clicks on his radio and tells his colleague the suspect must be feeding him a line. "She says she bought the house ten months ago and no car was sold on the property."

"I'm not surprised to hear this car story," I tell Wilson. "The neighbors have complained that Michael hung out with unsavory types. They did *not* like his friends at all."

The officer nods, apologizes again, and leaves for good this time.

I immediately call my real estate agent, Marina. From previous conversations I knew she had listed the house for Michael three years before my purchase. A buyer had made an offer and the house was put under contract, but Michael changed his mind at the last minute, despite having to pay a hefty penalty to back out of the deal. He claimed he couldn't handle the stress of selling and moving at that point in his life. During the house sale, Michael's ex-partner confided to Marina that Michael had serious mental health and addiction problems. He battled alcoholism and schizophrenia, though none of the neighbors were certain which condition came first.

Michael was found dead in a motel room during the spring of 2012, the year before I bought the house. He'd been visiting assisted living facilities in western Oregon to find a place with supportive care. Was he so depressed over the prospect of having to enter one of these places that he took his own life, as some suspected? Or was it an accidental overdose, a medical crisis? Whatever the case, it remains a mystery to the people with whom I've spoken.

Michael's ghost haunts me in this house, like the lingering acute anguish he must have suffered during the latter years of his decline. Michael, the accomplished artist. Michael, the flamboyant gay man. Michael, the noisy neighbor. Michael, adorer of roses. Michael, the pathetic drunk. Michael, the insane.

When I first visited the house, a Cape Cod cottage built in 1952, the furnishings were still in place. Traditional, ornate décor included a rose-velvet wing chair and an antique clock in the living room, and a rococo bedroom lamp. Michael's paintings covered the walls. He painted abstract landscapes which, on close inspection, showed tiny dots that reminded me of the Australian aboriginal style. When I'd asked Marina about his use of dots, she mentioned something about "painting by numbers." I looked up painting with dots and found two possibilities, *pointillism* and *ben-day dots*, but I couldn't decide if he used either. Through Marina, I'd conveyed a wish to buy one of the paintings from Michael's estate, but his family took them all away.

The neighbors welcomed me profusely. "We are *soooo* glad to have you here. You know, Michael . . . had problems."

At first, they described the problems obliquely. He was a boozer. He was mentally ill. He caused disturbances and was well known to the police. Each chat seemed to veer into a catharsis of Michael's transgressions, like a post-traumatic discharge of emotions. I learned Michael often wore brightly colored silk kimonos outdoors. Other times he appeared in gold see-thru shirts, a green sombrero, or striped satin shorts. Once he watered his roses wearing only a blue velvet jacket, leading neighbor Carl to angrily shout, "I have children, for God's sake!" He gave an unwanted kiss to one guy, who then slugged him. He played blaring music at all hours of the night. When a neighbor walked over at two a.m. and asked him to turn down the volume, Michael told her to "Fuck off." He walked through people's backyards without permission ("What are you doing here, Michael?" . . . "Just taking a shortcut."). He was a belligerent nuisance.

A few people mentioned that Michael tended to stand too close to the person he was talking to, and his aggressive "in your face" manner was unsettling.

Another neighbor related the sad story of going to a party at Michael's house. She and her housemate arrived on time, and the two women and Michael waited and waited, but no other guests showed. Michael got very drunk. This same neighbor told me Michael threw what appeared to be pieces of junk out on his lawn. "It's possible, though, that these were actually intended to be art projects," she added.

After the officer leaves, my curiosity leads me to Michael's online blog, something I've avoided out of fear of filling my brain with disturbing images. Little did I know Michael considered himself a rare genius. He described himself as "a self-taught theoretical nuclear physicist" who beat Einstein himself at least twelve times at his own game. Moreover, Michael was convinced "beyond doubt" that he personified "some unusual, exotic transmitter to the greater universe," one who had become "a genuine historical person like Socrates, Aristotle, Buddha, Jesus, Mohammed, Galileo, Newton [and] Picasso."

Lest I latch onto a caricature of a madman, I remind myself that Michael must have functioned successfully at one time. He'd earned two degrees from Reed College, a BA in Political Science and a Master of Teaching with a specialization in art. Curiously, I'd found one of his Reed diplomas on the kitchen counter when I moved in. According to a neighbor, he had classically trained in art, and three of his paintings hung in the halls of Reed at one time. According to his blog, however, Michael Hewitt seemed most proud of the fact he was "completely & absolutely self-taught in theoretical nuclear physics," which enabled him to make grand contributions to knowledge. From what I pieced together, his employment history was unstable, and he worked a variety of jobs over the years.

The charismatic nature of Michael's personality intrigues me. A journalist passing through town had met Michael in a bar and spent hours in conversation with him. He published an article titled "Michael of the Sparkly Eyes," which could be ordered at one time through Amazon. When I check the retailer's website, the title was listed as no longer available. I had imagined that sparkly eyes meant naturally incandescent irises, but I had to laugh when someone later told me Michael loved to wear glitter eyeshadow.

When I see in Michael's blog that he ran for mayor of Portland, I think the claim must be bogus. To my surprise, not only was he on the ballot, but the unlikely candidate garnered eighty-seven votes. The neighbors did say he had a lot of friends, but these associates didn't seem like the voting type. Later, I learn Michael had thrice attempted to win the mayoral seat.

A website featuring "oddballs" running for mayor in 2012 described Michael as "a man who holds proof of God's existence" and who beat Einstein by applying

$e=mc^2$ to the human body. An online radio interview with fringe candidates allows me to hear Michael's voice—in itself unsettling, like he's speaking from the ether. Soft and clear, he outlines plans for Portland's economic development. One venture involves selling roses at Washington Park. He also champions the need to improve mental health services and the training of law enforcement to deal with the mentally ill.

My neighbor Carl relates stories about his mother's interactions with Michael. She'd befriended the artist and purchased one of his paintings. One day Michael asked Carl's mother, "On a scale of one to ten, how crazy do you think I am?" The woman turned the question back on him, asking, "Well, what do *you* think, Michael?"

He thought for a minute. "I'd give myself a twelve."

From his blog I learn Michael had self-published a nineteen-page booklet guaranteed "to change your outlook, your mind and your entire life," by applying his theories of nuclear physics to tackle issues such as low self-esteem. The booklet, available at a local new age bookstore, could be purchased through Michael's blog using PayPal. In fact, the reader is encouraged throughout the blog to make donations to his cause.

An early blog entry deplores the mistreatment Michael suffered at the hands of a local store manager, who allegedly called him an "old queer" for giving him the "evil eye." Michael was asked to leave after attempting to buy a handmade tin candle holder. Michael's repeated calls to management led to a home visit by the Portland police to advise him that he'd better stop calling the store.

What a troubled life this poor man had led. Living in his house, I feel burdened by the memory of his suffering. Could it affect my psyche, I wonder? Given the intense feelings his presence in the neighborhood evoked, will his memory affect how the neighbors see me?

In time, the house and yard reveal more clues to the mystery of Michael Hewitt. Described as a "fixer-upper," years of neglect had turned the backyard into a jungle, and the rooms inside the house look sad and dingy. As I explore the storage space in the attic a few weeks after moving in, a small box catches my attention. I pull it out to examine the contents, and my eyes grow wide reading the titles of old magazines—*Mandate, Inches, Men, Bunkhouse, Honcho, Jock*. Oh my, I say to myself, a vintage gay porn collection. There are issues from the 1970s to the 2000s, the hairstyles following the decades. One magazine, *Hombres Latinos*, is in Spanish, and I notice a page marker. Flipping to the page, the name MICHAEL HEWITT jumps off the caption next to a nude photo. *Oh noooo*, I think, *it's him*! I slam the rag shut. The last thing I want in my head is an erotic image of Michael. Instead, I want to feel compassion, so I can rest at ease in the space he occupied for seven years.

What to do with the cache? I wonder if a collector might be interested. Maybe there are websites to sell this stuff. Or perhaps I should just throw it out. Undecided, I return the box to its hiding place.

As I try to forget about Michael, my neighbors continue to bring up his atrocious behavior and how happy they are to have me living there instead. I feel a certain pressure to provide a benevolent antidote to my predecessor's distasteful legacy. I can only hope that in time, I will validate their expectations of my upstanding character, and they will relax about the past. To this end I remain vigilant about avoiding negative impressions, regularly posing questions to myself about how my actions might appear to observers. Am I maintaining my front yard to acceptable standards? Do I seem like too much of a homebody? When I begin hosting snuggle parties for friends through the Meetup group, I imagine observers may wonder why people are bringing pillows inside. Once, my nosey next-door neighbor comments, "Hey, I'm glad to see you had a party," seeming to be fishing for more details. I demur, saying, "Yes, the party turned out great. Everyone had a good time."

When the next venting session occurs in my driveway, I seize the occasion to find out more about Michael.

"Do you know if Michael identified as Hispanic?" I ask.

"Not that I know of," one neighbor responds, and the others agree.

"Why do you ask?"

"In some of the photos I've seen, he looks like he might be Latino," I explain, not wanting to go into details.

That leads me to look again in *Hombres* to see if the man looks Latino. Hard to tell. Then I realize the credit says *photographed* by Michael Hewitt, so maybe he isn't the guy posing with an erection after all. But the model is also identified as "Michael," so did he photograph himself in the mirror? Months later, writing this story, I'll check the index of the magazine and learn that Michael the model is different from Michael the photographer. Phew! I had not seen his genitals.

Meanwhile, the taming of the jungle continues. When I moved in, the overgrown back hedge and other shrubs covered a third of the yard. The landscaper had to cut back everything, exposing large patches of bare earth, like a lawn stripped down to its underwear. In one unsightly section, Michael had dumped scores of tiny paint vials in the dirt. Curiously, dozens of house-type keys dotted the soil with the vials. What doors had they opened, I wondered. Now, tired of looking at the mess, I begin collecting the paints and keys to put in the trash. I notice a piece of black plastic sticking out of the ground behind the garage. When I tug, it doesn't budge, so I dig around it with a shovel. Something wrapped in a small garbage bag had been buried about a foot underground.

I carry the bag onto the back deck to look inside. "Wow," I exclaim softly. Stacks of photographic slides, only slightly damaged in their plastic sleeves, fill the bag. Michael, it seems, was quite the porn photographer. Buried in the dirt was a collection of about 100 slides depicting the male anatomy from different angles and in varying states of erection. I take the bag inside to go through the contents slowly. That's when I find the consent forms his models had signed to pose for the photos. *Oh, damn, I have the names of these people.*

Again, I ask myself, what should I do with this stuff? Put it in the trash? Michael apparently didn't want to do that. I simply put the bag away, undecided.

I feel sure there is more to discover about the enigma of Michael Hewitt. Perhaps those house keys hold a clue. It occurs to me that if Michael had keys to other people's homes, perhaps others might also be in possession of keys to his house. After all, not long ago someone felt bold enough to tell a police officer he bought a car from Michael's driveway.

Around that time, I notice the disappearance of several items from my home. A portable phone, a book, my reading glasses. Did someone sneak in and take them as a prank? That certainly would fit with the stories I'd been told . . . .

Time to change the locks.

Weeks later, I find the missing items upstairs, on the newly carpeted floor I'd lain on to test its softness as a cuddling platform.

Over the next few years, no new clues surface about Michael. Slowly, I relinquish thoughts of the tortured artist, the neighbors stop berating him, and I claim the house as my own. I take pride in the renovations I've completed and enjoy inhabiting the cheerful rooms. For the first time, I have my own wood-burning fireplace and savor the warmth, crackle and flames of a comforting fire. The specter of Michael stays at bay for two years, but when chicken raising disrupts my sanity, my thoughts return to Michael's madness. Could the house be cursed? Not someone to give credence to the occult, I quickly dismiss such thoughts when they intrude.

I write this story about Michael and share it with my writing group, feeling a twinge of guilt. Am I paying a psychological price for revealing his life? I'd changed his name but a good sleuth might piece together his identity.

I wrestle with these questions off and on as I recover from the emotional breakdown of chicken keeping and establish a meditation practice. In the end, I decide Michael would relish the attention of having his remarkable story told.

When I prepare to sell the house after living in it more than four years, I finally dispose of the pornographic relics. I give the magazines to an appreciative collector, turn the consent forms into ash, and bury the slides in the local landfill.

ROSE CITY AUDITION

Snuggling with Peers

A foot rested in my lap, and I had no idea to whom it belonged. I nestled in a "puppy pile," the cozy assortment of people who snuggle together at a cuddle party. With lights dimmed, eyes closed, and heads resting on pillows, we occasionally talked or laughed or even fell asleep, but mostly we basked in the comfort of tactile bliss. Later, we regrouped into a spooning formation, one arm draped over the side of the person in front. Along the edges of the living room, more people snuggled in pairs and trios. These clusters of overlapping limbs and torsos morphed for a couple of hours before the party ended, our touch needs sated for the evening.

I'd joined the Meetup group Touch Positive Oregon even before moving to Portland, so excited was I to find the kind of peer touch group I'd fantasized about for a long time. For me, the hardest part about living as a single person over many years was the acute sense of touch deprivation from never being held affectionately. Our society enforces strict taboos on adult touch outside of romantic relationships. When I attended a small, intimate cuddle party in someone's living room, only six seeks after arriving in Portland, I couldn't believe my good fortune. Being held in someone's arms sent a rush of feel-good endorphins through my body and etched a blissful smile across my face. A comforting sensation of nurturing warmth suffused my being throughout the evening, and I left the party feeling collectively embraced by a dozen kind-hearted people.

Following my initial foray into cuddling, I attended a Rub and Grub, which combined a potluck in one room with massage from several pairs of hands in another. Soon after, I found myself at Free Hugs Day at the Farmers Market and at cuddle parties with themes: game nights, movie nights, beach snuggles, and Cuddle Cafés, complete with menus offering tactile selections. But mostly I enjoyed the simple cuddle parties where the focus was on lots of hugging. After these incredibly soothing encounters, I slept like a baby.

The touch group became my primary social network in Portland for the first three years. In time I began hosting snuggle parties in the upstairs space of my Sellwood home and took an informal leadership role in the group. I envisioned myself as a pioneer and champion of this bold new movement. I had found my cause.

Although the peer touch movement has roots in counterculture groups of the 1960s, it gained renewed interest in recent years through the emergence of snuggle parties and professional cuddlers to meet the needs of single adults and others without access to affectionate touch. Proponents of the touch movement hail the benefits of touch, including: reduced heart rate, blood pressure, and the stress hormone cortisol; an increase in the "love hormone" oxytocin; and mitigation of the effects of touch deprivation—depression, sleep disturbance, anger, violence, eating disorders, and lower immune function.

Having easy access to snuggle groups in Portland often felt too good to be true. I remembered the negative reactions I'd received in the spring of 2012 when I presented an essay titled "Touch Hunger" to a writing group in Tampa, a city that had no touch groups. In the essay I argued in favor of *touch support groups* to meet the needs of touch-deprived adults. I had not yet heard of snuggle parties, but I envisioned similar gatherings. My fellow writers roundly dismissed the idea as socially unacceptable.

"It won't fly," they said. "Our society isn't ready for that."

When later that year I found myself snuggling with strangers in a Portland living room, I felt vindicated. It struck me as a good example of how culture change evolves differently across the regions of our country.

When I shared my experiences with one of my Louisiana relatives, she responded: "You really *are* weird."

Even though I found pockets of acceptance in Portland where touch groups flourish, some members of my writing group expressed skepticism about gaining social approval for peer touch. Anything you write about it, they cautioned, should clearly state at the very beginning that cuddle groups are not about sex, because without such a disclaimer, people will assume otherwise and may stop reading.

When the very conventional mainstream publication *AARP The Magazine* ran a story in December 2015 about touch needs of seniors, describing cuddle parties in a positive light, I cheered. *It's happening*, I thought. Peer cuddling is slowly becoming an everyday thing, not just for the adventurous. And when Disney presented otters having a cuddle party in the 2016 movie *Finding Dory*, snuggling seemed to be going mainstream. But despite the growing positive coverage in the media, it remains uncertain how widely peer touch will be accepted in American society.

My experience in the touch community of Portland underscores two major challenges to legitimation of snuggling: the persistent association of peer touch with sexuality, and the pejorative image of people who attend snuggle events as psychosocially deficient in some way.

The wariness toward touch events felt by many

people stems partly from the larger society's taboos about nonromantic touch, and partly from the touch community's association with sex-positive subcultures, an assortment of social movements that embrace all aspects of sexuality as healthy and pleasurable. Overlapping membership among touch and sex-positive groups is common. People who practice polyamory (having multiple intimate relationships with mutual consent), for example, and people comfortable with open sexual relationships, often make up the early participants drawn to snuggle parties.

In Portland, an organization called LoveTribe paved the way for the emergence of a vibrant touch community through its sponsorship of events offering gradations of intimacy. The group invented terminology for different "levels" of intimacy that have become widely used. *Snuggle parties* designate exclusively platonic touch, *romps* are sensual events where upper body nudity and kissing, but no direct genital contact, are allowed, and *eros* events involve full sexual participation. Touch Positive Oregon evolved from this group during a period when LoveTribe was inactive, initially sponsoring both platonic events and romps, although the latter, surprisingly, were publicized as platonic in nature. Following a change in leadership and a somewhat contentious internal debate, Touch Positive Oregon discontinued romps and began holding exclusively platonic cuddle parties. It also changed its name to Oregon Touch (OT) to distance itself from the sex-positive movement.

As an anthropologist with many years studying both support groups and social stigma, I worried about the public image of the new touch group in Portland. In the early days before the policy change, I chafed at the discrepancy between the way the group labeled itself as platonic on its Meetup homepage, and yet advertised "juicy" events where "light making out" and going topless were allowed. I expressed my concerns to one of the organizers and she promised to talk to the leadership about it, but I never heard back. Later, someone at an event asked a leader to define platonic. Her definition included romp-style activities. I jumped in to advocate for eliminating sensual events in service to the larger good of societal acceptance. "Members are free to decline to participate in any activities that make them uncomfortable," she countered.

People in Portland's touch community often argued that participation in any event was *consensual*, as if the voluntary nature of an activity should obviate any concerns one might have about it. There didn't seem to be an awareness of the impact of social perceptions on peer touch as a movement.

By the time I started hosting snuggle parties in my upstairs space, there were clear rules in place to guide acceptable, nonsexual behavior. New members were required to attend an Introduction to Snuggling class that addressed norms, boundaries, and consent. Clothing was never optional. At the start of a cuddle session, participants introduced themselves as either "puppies" or "cats," stating whether they were open to snuggling with anyone without first being asked for permission (a puppy) or whether they preferred to be asked before someone initiated touching (a cat).

In June 2014 I hosted my first event with ten people in attendance. *Touch Talk* consisted of a discussion group plus cuddle session. I wanted to share ideas about how groups like ours could play an advocacy role in society to promote greater acceptance of organized touch events. In particular, we explored ways to desexualize common misperceptions of snuggle parties. Animated talk focused on a recurrent theme—how to mainstream touch groups by increasing community awareness and holding events in public places. The Free Hugs events at the Farmers Market are an example of these kinds of normalization processes. We talked about how decades ago, massage therapy went through a similar legitimation process, in which the profession disassociated itself from the shady massage parlors of old. Touch groups face similar challenges in shedding their identification with erotic activities. I also shared with the group my perspective that societal taboos against nonromantic touch deny single people access to the full range of physical affection. Bella

DePaulo, a psychologist who has written extensively on discrimination against single adults, calls such marginalization *singlism*. Taboos against nonromantic touch place an unnecessary burden on uncoupled people to find specialized sources of touch.

Following *Touch Talk*, I began hosting monthly snuggle parties, mostly in the evening and typically lasting about three hours, with eight to fifteen people present. I had fixed up my upstairs into a snuggle den with foam mattresses, pillows, and blankets providing the *fluff* to cushion our bodies. These gatherings continued through Fall of 2015, when a growing problem posed a new challenge for the group—retention of members. Over time we'd noticed an increasing turnover among people who attended the snuggle parties. New people continued to join the Meetup and attend an introductory class, but they often tried only one or two events and didn't return. The gatherings became largely a collection of strangers, each time a new set of faces and personalities to get to know.

To better understand why people were not returning for more events, the group's founder Kristen queried members about what might be causing this turnover. She discovered that people were satisfied with the kind of events offered and the forms of cuddling available, but they felt uncomfortable with the strangeness of some of the participants. They said many of the people seemed "weird" to them in some way and hard to relate to. Kristen described the pattern as reminiscent of high school notions of popular and unpopular crowds. Popular people, she explained, shy away from parties where unpopular people predominate. Listening to this analysis, I felt sad that these old patterns from our early years still affected us in adult life (even in a city that prides itself for being *weird*!).

The social compatibility theory rang true to me. At events I hosted and many others, a disproportionate number of individuals who attended would be considered, by mainstream society, oddball characters, socially awkward, or strange. Oregon Touch seemed to attract introverts, geeks, people recovering from addictions and mental illness, veterans with PTSD, physically less able persons, transgender folks, and others who might make a straight, "normal" crowd uncomfortable.

In *The Snuggle Party Guidebook*,[2] Dave Wheitner notes that touch events tend to attract people who have difficulty relating to others, such as those on the autism spectrum, and who seek opportunities for nurturing touch in a structured setting. Since I place myself somewhere on the spectrum, I took pride in providing a venue for safe touch that is welcoming to neurodiverse individuals. But such openness can have a downside—neurotypical people may feel ill at ease.

To counteract the turnover phenomenon, we tried different scenarios. Kristen and I implemented a strategy to assemble a stable group of people that met on a regular basis and got to know one another, so instead of greeting new faces each time, participants embraced the same people every month, over time building trust and caring. The announcement billed the group as open to anyone but noted that after a couple of meetings it would be closed, with new members added by invitation only. Thus, the Friends Friday Night Snuggle was born.

For the first few months, the formula seemed to work. Meeting the first Friday of the month in my snuggle den, the group sustained a core membership of about a dozen people who learned one another's names; as members drifted away, others were added one at a time. After a few months, however, attendance began to decline, and eventually we suspended the group for lack of interest.

Faced with declining attendance at events and competition from other organizations sponsoring touch events, in the summer of 2016 Oregon Touch entered another transition. It sought to merge with one of the more successful of these organizations, called SnuggleHQ, which had been hosting platonic snuggle parties for two years and seemed to be attracting more participants. This group operated as an entrepreneurial business, with a website, Snuggle Mobile, and fee-based events.

Participation in SnuggleHQ events was selective;

not everyone who applied was accepted. Disclaimers such as the following accompanied publicity for events: "Due to the need to create a thoughtful mix of attendees, our RSVP Manager will follow up asap to notify you if you're on the final guest list." Presumably the composition of a "thoughtful mix" included demographics and experience with cuddling, but the rubric for a "thoughtful mix" wasn't defined, leaving open the possibility that personality traits such as introversion or social competence also came into play, in order to limit the number of socially awkward attendees.

When I asked the founder of SnuggleHQ what niche she sought to fill with her snuggle parties that wasn't already served by Oregon Touch, she said her impression of our events was that they were "introverted," and she wanted to offer more playful gatherings with a party-like atmosphere, where participants were encouraged to wear theme-focused costumes to help create a festive ambience. Her first two snuggle events after taking over the Meetup included a Pirate and Gypsy Snuggle and a Zombie Snuggle.

The new fee structure for events privileged couples by offering a discount for signing up with a friend, and, with a nod to polyamory, three people could economize even more by registering as a "pod."

SnuggleHQ also reverted to the original LoveTribe levels of intimacy framework and began to offer more sexual events along with cuddle parties. Participants at both platonic and sexual events were asked to sign an 867-word legal waiver releasing the organizers from liability for, among other things, someone contracting a sexually transmitted infection. Consequently, even people interested in attending platonic-only events had to read about sexual behavior and sign a document agreeing to disclose their sexual health to others.

Many members of OT didn't see a problem with an organization offering both platonic and sexual forums. They argued that if the rules for different sessions are clearly stated, people can decide for themselves which activities fall within their comfort zones. While I understood their point, I believe the general public doesn't make such fine distinctions. To continue the massage analogy, just imagine if in the early days of legitimizing massage therapy as a health profession, a business advertised itself as providing therapeutic massage during the day, and sexual massage after hours. The mere existence of such a duality would taint all massage practice and stymie efforts to change its image.

SnuggleHQ soon changed its name to Conscious Touch NW and adopted an expanded mission to promote the full range of sex-positive events. Romps and Eros events were advertised under the banner "Sensual Playground Presents," a name elsewhere associated with a Playgirl porn film.

We'd come full circle, I realized, and the battle to preserve nonsexual peer touch in Portland had been lost. An organization that initially sought to distance itself from the sex-positive movement had morphed into a vehicle for its celebration. I felt deflated. When I met with the new leader to explain my opposition to these changes, she made a sincere pitch for the healthfulness of a broad sex-positive agenda to promote the redefinition of human sexuality as encompassing all forms of affective touch, including platonic snuggle parties as well as newborn babies needing to be held. She saw her work as that of an activist for normalizing sex-positive values.

"Would it make you feel better knowing that the sensual and sexual events are heart-centered?" she asked me.

"No, it wouldn't," I replied.

The story of Oregon Touch is an example of an organization evolving over time and ultimately returning to its roots as a sex-positive entity, one that has integrated (some might say co-opted) snuggling into its purview. There is money to be made in snuggle events, and even more profit potential in romps and sex parties. As always, Portland is teeming with would-be entrepreneur-activists primed to capitalize on the latest wave of self-development trends.

With a heavy heart I left the group that had given me cherished moments of affective touch as well as hope for the legitimation of peer touch in mainstream society. I didn't want to contribute to an organization that harmed the larger mission of destigmatizing touch.

My greatest hope is that peer touch groups will become widely available to meet the needs of touch-deprived adults and that singles, introverts and other marginalized people inevitably drawn to them will be afforded a welcoming place of quiet, comforting touch without having to don a costume.

ROSE CITY AUDITION

The Oregon Country Fair

Every July, thousands of revelers flock to the Oregon Country Fair, the long-running countercultural gathering near Eugene. Local informants tout the fair as the epitome of the Oregon cultural experience. "You must see it at least once," a trustworthy friend advised. "It's the ultimate hippie gathering anywhere. Been going on since the sixties. The sights and sounds will bowl you over."

In the spring of 2015, I find a colorful insert for the fair in *The Portland Mercury* depicting brightly costumed merrymakers and immediately begin making plans to go. The event website promises abundant enjoyment from scores of musicians at multiple stages, as well as a dedicated dance pavilion with performances throughout the day. There will be delectable foods and hundreds of booths and vendors featuring everything imaginative, creative, and quirky.

The line of vehicles inching toward the entrance to the fair stretches a mile and a half. This slow crawl, after driving more than two hours on highways, provides a welcome respite and allows for people-watching in the campsites along the way. In one campground, a spectacularly colorful bus occupies a place of honor. I later learn this is the second incarnation of Ken Kesey's famous psychedelic bus from his sixties road trip with the Merry Pranksters.

In keeping with the name, the fairgrounds are located in the country. Cars pour into a huge field and park in hand-numbered rows. As I make the long walk to the entrance, I pass other parking fields, already filled. I begin to suspect there will be a lot of people inside the venue. Mild apprehension arises.

Once through the entrance, I assume the dense throngs of people will thin out as I wander deeper. Not the case. Along every narrow pathway jam-packed with bodies, slow rivulets of foot traffic snake along. No open spaces appear anywhere, even at the main stage, which boasts a large expanse of ground for lounging on blankets. Later, I'll learn more than twenty thousand people, a record crowd, attended the fair that day. Over the three days of the fair, attendance of forty-five thousand is typical.

The press of people makes it difficult to appreciate the spectacular body art, costumes, and adornment on display. Given the family-friendly atmosphere, the occasional sight of women's bare breasts surprises me. The carnival atmosphere feels frenetic, as if fairgoers are impelled to keep moving and absorb everything in view, never stopping because no places to sit or stand can be found. Laid out in labyrinthine form, the long lanes are difficult to navigate, especially for a first timer. Feeling claustrophobic and disoriented, I sympathize with parents straining to push strollers carrying sweaty, overstimulated kids. Unlike me, however, everyone around seems to be genuinely enjoying themselves.

In the dance pavilion, I feel lucky landing a seat on a bale of hay and watch a group of differently abled dancers perform. This newly built venue affords more breathing room than the older sections. Afterward, I can't pass up the opportunity to tour a tiny house on display. It reminds me of the memoir I'd read by a Portland woman who built her own little house.

Back into the human stream to find food, I stop at a burrito stand, miraculously finding room to eat standing up facing a wooden shelf. Less fortunate patrons hastily gulp their food without benefit of seat, table, or shelf.

I wander aimlessly through the maze, occasionally encountering a rag-tag parade of people in flamboyant attire playing drums and brass instruments. A group of young cellists finish a piece at the Youth Stage. The rest of my day blurs into kaleidoscope images of tie-died shirts, painted skin, music, circus acts, and pungent aromas. Endless rows of stalls displaying countless wares bring to mind a folk festival on steroids.

I find myself desperately seeking the exit. I have

to escape not just the press of the crowds but the disquieting sense of unreality permeating the entire event, like when a dream turns into a nightmare of funhouse distortions. Not a good setting for someone on the autism spectrum.

The prior week I'd read Christian Lander's satirical book, *Stuff White People Like*. I mentally compose a new entry— "White people are nuts about festivals, particularly those with themes harking back to the sixties or the Renaissance era. They love fairs with a wholesome, family-friendly ambience of progressive good taste, where people dress up in costumes and colorful outfits. The more rules and orderliness of the event, the better, such as taboos on alcohol, drugs, videotaping, and full nudity. White people want to experience the illusion of wanton abandon found in festivals of old, all the while feeling secure in the decorous comfort of the controlled familiar." Upon further reflection, I decide my entry describes Americans in general, not just white people.

Would my experience differ in a less crowded environment? Probably yes, given my low threshold for overstimulation. Even with fewer people, however, the fair still would seem larger than life, the performance of a central ritual of American culture, the summer festival. Like their compatriots in other states, Oregonians must attend at least one festival during the warm weather months. The Oregon

Country Fair indeed exemplifies local culture, a genuine artifact of home-grown entertainment fit for the folksy as well as the hip. But the festival also partakes of a much larger tradition.

Despite my unease and sense of unreality about the fair, I have accomplished an important seasonal duty. I have made the pilgrimage to Oregon's summer festival and survived to write about it.

ROSE CITY AUDITION

I write satire to keep sane. And, hopefully, to make people laugh. I mentally tame the absurdity of the world around me through humor, parody, sarcasm, and hyperbole. The following three essays served this purpose at various points in my sojourn. They are best enjoyed by not trying to figure out what is actually true about Portland.

Mahonia aquifolium *blossom, the Oregon state flower, abundantly found in the understory of Douglas firs.*

Docent Corps Takes Portland

A new Portlander told me, "Have you tried to get into Habitat for Humanity? It's a closed group. Slots are filled months in advance and your only hope is to sub for an occasional cancellation."

During my training as a tour guide for a botanical garden in Portland, our instructor encouraged us to upgrade our status to that of a *docent*, like you find in museums and art galleries. This enhancement included using scientific names for plants instead of common names. The first time I used the term *Mahonia aquifolium* with a tour group, a few people snickered. Nevertheless, I committed to properly perform my role, whether the unschooled liked it or not. So, a few months later, when Portland launched its Master Docent® Program, with only thirty privileged candidates to be accepted into the inaugural class, I applied immediately.

Like similar programs around the country that produce Master Gardeners, Master Composters, and Master Recyclers, the Master Docent Program is designed to appropriate idle time from retirees and ecozealots in order to staff public programs starved for funding. According to the Corporation for National and Community Service, Portland ranked sixth in the nation for volunteerism in 2014, behind Salt Lake City, Minneapolis, Milwaukee, Charlotte, and Rochester. Portlanders can breathe a sigh of relief that Seattle moved down to seventh place after beating out the Rose City the previous year. Regardless, why does Seattle, with its exorbitant sales tax, need so many volunteers to run the city, anyway?

Ever committed to staying on the cutting edge, Portland is the first city in the country to establish a Master Docent Program. Envisioned as an elite corps of gracious and knowledgeable guides, screening and training for the docents is selective, rigorous, and expensive. While it costs participants a mere fifty dollars for the privilege of being trained as a Master Recycler, for example, aspiring docents gladly cough up five hundred to become an MD. No one dares question the price tag, because doing so might reflect poorly on their loyalty and commitment.

The selection process begins with a twenty-page online application covering one's life history, employment experience, hobbies, general health, and medium-term goals, such as, "Where do you see yourself in five years?" Next, an in-depth psychological assessment weeds out introverts, pessimists, anarchists, substance abusers, and other social misfits. Desirable personality traits, on the other hand, such as talkativeness, self-confidence, assertiveness, and exceptional friendliness, are rated highly. New arrivals to Portland need not apply. To be eligible to become a Master Docent, one must have lived in Portland at least five years. In addition, requirements include having previously volunteered at least one hundred hours in each of three different "Master" type programs, preferably in Oregon. Lastly, the applicant must commit to attending weekly training sessions for twenty-five weeks. Absences are excused only for deaths in the family and emergency volunteering for an approved organization.

Those applicants who successfully meet the selection criteria are then scheduled for an audition. They choose a real-life, nonprofit organization, and a scenario is made up to represent a typical encounter with a visitor. Judges observe the applicant interacting with a simulated guest, rating the performance on qualities such as sincerity of smile, enthusiasm, spontaneity, engagement, and thoroughness of message. Impressive scores on the audition qualify the applicant to be accepted into the Master Docent Program.

The training itself covers the usual topics, such as how to maintain eye contact with a visitor across the room who may have glanced in your direction but has not yet decided to walk over and be guided. The important thing is to avoid letting the guest get away without the benefit of your finely tuned and well-rehearsed spiel. Once the target has moved within range, you must do everything in your power to get them to agree to the tour. Polite excuses are easily brushed aside, but the more serious obstacles, such as "I prefer to visit the exhibit on my own," require more creative tactics. "Oh, of course, I understand, but are you aware that loners have a shorter life expectancy than extroverts?" Paramount importance is accorded ensnaring the target before a mere volunteer, who is not part of the elite corps, gets to them first. You see, stiff competition exists among civic programs in the number of people contacts and hours worked by its volunteers.

Creative strategies have evolved to enhance the encounter, especially when there are more volunteers present than needed, which is not uncommon. One approach is to have two docents perform a duet with a single visitor, trading off seamlessly in reciting the litany of relevant facts. By using two stones to hit a single bird, the contact tally is doubled in one fell swoop. Questioning the necessity of acting out such a duet risks getting an official censure for lack of team spirit.

Some volunteer activities, of course, can only be performed by one person at a time. Take mending garments at a repair event, for example. It's very difficult to have more than one person operating a sewing machine. Sadly, it's been tried. I recall one event where I arrived early to set up and be ready to go when the first client appeared. Meanwhile, five other volunteers set up their machines on either side of me. When the first customers arrived, somehow the jobs were distributed to everyone except me. Seething with frustration I announced loudly, "I can't believe I was the first volunteer here and don't have anything to fix." The other women only smirked and shrugged as they hoarded their work. Later on, we learned how to increase mending volume by encouraging people to bring in their pet's garments.

Another component of training prepares docents to handle the organization's Church Lady. The Church Lady may be a staff member or a volunteer. His or her job is to know all the ins and outs of the organization and to position herself in a gatekeeping role so everyone, even those at the highest levels, must deal with her to get things done. I once made the mistake of asking the volunteer coordinator if the Church Lady could boss me around. Rather than confront the matter directly, the supervisor wisely handed my query to the Executive Director, who deftly said a bunch of things that left the matter ambiguous. Church Ladies routinely put volunteers through rites of subordination, but Master Docents, lest they get airs of superiority, are singled out for swift and decisive domination. Being mentally prepared for such maneuvers helps the MD get along with the Church Lady without directly challenging her authority.

The first Master Docent class graduated with much fanfare. Portland Mayor Charlie Hales presented the coveted ID badges shaped like the city of Portland. In his remarks, Hales praised the work of all the city's volunteers: "Our great city would grind to a halt were it not for the free labor provided by its generous citizens." He also announced some exciting new programs, including Master Dumpster Divers and Master Bottle Collectors, designed to especially benefit the homeless population. Still other programs under development are the Master Protester class, Master Hipster training, and even a Doctorate in Volunteering. With such diverse opportunities at our disposal, surely Portland will soon take its rightful place as the most volunteering city in the USA.

ROSE CITY AUDITION

Smile Your Way to Success

My inspiration for this satire was a laughter yoga class where trained instructors led us through a series of exercises designed to elicit uncontrollable laughter. It worked!

Hold onto your lips, folks — the hottest trend in self-improvement has arrived. Smile shaping is taking the country by storm, and classes can't keep up with demand.

What the heck is smile shaping, you may be asking yourself. With roots in ethology, the science of animal behavior, smile shaping uses systematic exercises to train people to use various forms of smiling to meet challenging social situations. For example: want to cast a malicious smirk in the direction of your nemesis? Or perhaps don a flirtatious grin to attract that hottie across the room? Then smile shaping is just the thing for you.

While some observers view smile shaping as an offshoot of laughter yoga, others maintain it has closer affinity with career counseling. Like laughter yoga, smile shaping builds on the principle that your brain can't distinguish between genuine and mimicked emotion. Fake laughter has the same beneficial effects on your body as natural laughter, and likewise, fake smiles can produce the feelings associated with smiling. Also, following in the footsteps of laughter yoga with its clubs for practitioners, smile clubs have been popping up around the country.

However, the swiftness with which the corporate community and professional development gurus have adopted smile shaping accounts for its association with job performance. Being able to show the right smile for the occasion has become an essential skill for occupational success, similar to being tech savvy. And as a managerial tool, sending recalcitrant employees out for smile training is considered one of the most important breakthroughs in personnel management.

Through a series of exercises involving facial contortions, vocalization, and social interaction, trainees learn the basic repertoire of smiling: the goofy smile, the wistful smile, the come-hither, the sincere smile, the Mona Lisa, the maniacal smile, the ultimate smirk, the benevolent smile, the Shirley Temple (dimples not included), and many more. Proficient practitioners are able to instantly summon the perfect smile for any occasion, *while actually feeling the emotions behind it.* The potential benefits are seemingly limitless—being able to control one's moods through the mere contraction of muscles—what a breakthrough for psychotherapy and self-help!

Renowned smile shaping expert Dr. Houkares summed it up: "The principle of faking it in general has gained widespread popularity in the West. It's real if you believe it, dammit. Authenticity *can* be simulated!"

ROSE CITY AUDITION

Mindful Meddling

Book Review. By Still Waters. Awareness Press. $17.00

"If you're going to stick your nose in others' business, do it mindfully," opines celebrity life coach Still Waters in her latest best-seller, *Mindful Meddling*. The how-to guide takes nosiness to a new level, offering techniques for interfering in people's lives—for their own good, of course—in a focused, contemplative way. "They won't even realize what you're doing," she reassures readers. "Your ethereal demeanor will transfix them."

Mindful meddling adds yet another practice to the fast-growing field of *extreme mindfulness*, which already boasts mindful couponing, mindful boxing, and mindful AC repair. The key to success is concentration, whether you're running a finger along your sister's dusty surfaces or gently suggesting someone should lose weight. The important thing is to free your mind of extraneous thoughts and give undivided attention to the successful critique of others' lives.

In mindful meddling, nonverbal behavior is

important. It helps, for example, if you follow admonitions about calorie intake with a solemn bowing of the head (placing hands together at heart center is optional). This softens the impact of your words and makes it more difficult for the receiver to tell you to fuck off. Eye contact should only be broken at the moment you deliver the most offensive part of the message: "Don't you ever want to fit into your wedding dress again?"

Waters claims that, unlike ordinary meddlesomeness, mindful meddling is more effective in goading people to change. She offers step-by-step instructions on preparation, delivery, and damage control in the rare case of a botched intervention.

Testimonials from successful practitioners laud the method's effectiveness as a wholesome outlet for nefarious urges. As long as something is mindful, it must be noble.

"I used to interfere crudely," a grandfather confessed, "until I learned to do it with finesse, thanks to Waters' book."

"My friends can't believe the change in me," boasted a coed. "Instead of nagging in a whiney voice, now I intone softly, remembering to breathe deeply between intrusive remarks."

The book offers specialized scripts for mindfully meddling in common situations, such as getting one's neighbor to give up the comb-over, convincing a coworker to wear more stylish outfits, and stopping your best friend from breast-feeding her fiancé. For shy people, there's a whole chapter on "The Seven Stones of Non-Contact Meddling," like leaving a copy of the Alcoholism Self-Test, with great compassion, on your mother-in-law's counter. The book has even spawned online chat rooms where people share stories of shockingly intrusive prying that went off without a hitch, thanks to the helpful advice in this petite volume.

If your desire is to insinuate yourself, with loving kindness, joy, and equanimity, in the lives of those around you, this book is for you.

The Springwater Corridor

Many Portlanders develop a special relationship with one or more of its abundant green spaces—Forest Park, Hoyt Arboretum, Powell-Butte Nature Park, Oaks Bottom Wildlife Preserve—to name a few. My favorite retreat was the Springwater Corridor. This segment of the forty-mile loop around the metro area exemplifies some of the best and the worst of the Rose City, and I embraced it all.

I discovered the Springwater Corridor in 2012 when I called the Portland Parks and Recreation Department to ask where I could hike in the sun. The few parks I'd visited offered shady pathways beneath towering conifers, but I needed sunshine. Having lived near the shores of the Gulf of Mexico most of my life, including twenty-five years in the Sunshine State, Portland's seemingly endless overcast sky felt oppressive. On those rare days when the sun graced Portland with its welcome rays, I eagerly sought total exposure. The Corridor, I was told, had little shade. It could be accessed easily from my original neighborhood in the Far East, just off 122nd Avenue.

The Springwater Corridor got its name from an old railway line that parallels it. Opened in 1996, the asphalt trail stretches 21 miles along the southeast section of the loop, crossing Johnson Creek several times. The trail's ten-foot width accommodates two-way pedestrian and bicycle traffic. Cyclists tolerated the presence of pedestrians on the path but acted like they owned the road. Likewise, skaters and skateboarders zoomed around walkers with aplomb. Even I allowed myself to feel pleased when I passed pedestrians on my bike because they were the only people moving slower than me.

When I first accessed the trail, I focused on learning the wildflowers along the path. I photographed the ones I didn't recognize and showed the pictures to experts at Leach Botanical Garden, where I volunteered. There were many plants unfamiliar to me—California poppies, trillium, white irises, wild rose, elderberry, butterfly bush, teasel plant, fire weed. Like many areas of Oregon, the Corridor was heavily lined with the invasive Himalayan Blackberry that threatened native plants. Huge thickets of the shrub grew unchecked along many stretches. Gazing at the thorny bushes, I felt vaguely uneasy, worried the aggressive exotic would overtake the entire countryside. During blackberry season, however, I gladly joined the pickers with their buckets and made delicious sweet dough pies.

A big selling point for my Sellwood property was its proximity to the Springwater Corridor. A few blocks south of my street, heading east, a trail bridge crossed over a four-lane highway and railroad tracks before entering a green zone that included Tideman Johnson Park. The latter offered a scenic boardwalk over seasonal wetlands bordering the trail. Cottonwoods encircled a pond and carpeted the walkway with bright yellow, spade-shaped leaves in the fall. Next came lush vegetation, a ravine, brush, open fields, and streams. Where the trail crossed Johnson Creek, semi-circular overlooks allowed visitors to gaze down into the fast-moving water headed toward the Willamette River.

On the Corridor I didn't have to watch out for cars, traffic lights, curbs, and road signs. I could move along with ease, lost in thought or meditation. Once past the bridge over noisy McLoughlin Boulevard, things quieted down, birds flitted about, insects droned, and the air smelled fresher. The soft tinkling of a spring-fed stream joined the symphony. My breathing slowed. Warring thoughts of pending chores and stressful encounters subsided.

One of my favorite pastimes over the first two years was checking out the construction of the MAX light rail at Johnson Creek Station. The Corridor bridge over the tracks provided an excellent view of the site, as I keenly monitored the workers' progress at least once a week. Sometimes I took the side trail down to the edge of the construction site, a trail that would become a maintained path between the Corridor and the MAX. The grand opening of the Orange Line in September 2015 represented a big deal for the community where I lived. Sellwood residents would finally have access to light rail downtown and all parts of greater Portland.

Here and there benches flanked the Corridor. Near the boardwalk turnoff, two benches rested side by side in a pleasant, shady spot. A wooden canopy provided the only cover on my route. I liked to stop there to stretch my lower back. These same benches were frequented by a homeless man who had fashioned an impressive contraption for carrying his belongings. The lead conveyance was a bicycle, and to it were attached three consecutive bike trailers. All manner of gear and provisions were harnessed to the long rig, including two extra bicycles.

The first time I encountered the man, he sat on the bench, going through a stack of CDs. Curious about his amazing cart, I sat on the bench next to his and surreptitiously examined his possessions—mattress, stove, clothes, books, utensils.

"Hello, my name is Douglas," he said, startling me and reaching out to shake my hand. The man looked to be in his forties, clean and well-groomed. Surprised at his friendliness, I introduced myself, but didn't try to make conversation. Douglas continued to sort through his CDs.

He must have a battery-powered CD player in there somewhere, I thought. *It looks like he has everything but the kitchen sink, so why not music?*

Feeling like an intruder in his personal space, I didn't stay long. A few weeks later, I needed to find a home for a box of leftover sandwiches. *Maybe Douglas would appreciate them*, I thought, and headed for the trail. Sure enough, Douglas sat in his usual spot.

"Hi, Douglas. I went to a party last night and we had a bunch of sandwiches leftover." I opened the lid to show him what the food looked like. "Would you like to have them?"

"Sure," he said, "that'd be great. Thank you."

I handed him the box and said goodbye. On my return trip, I hoped Douglas had moved on so I wouldn't have to encounter him again. He sat there still. I just smiled and nodded as I rode by.

On future walks, I again found myself hoping Douglas wouldn't be sitting on the bench by the boardwalk so I could use it in solitude. Ungenerous thoughts surfaced like, *This guy has appropriated those benches like they're his home, depriving others of using them.* Then I'd catch myself and censor my thoughts. *The poor guy has no place to live; give him a break.*

Douglas was one of many homeless people who camped along the Springwater Corridor. The signs of occupation were everywhere—discarded sleeping bags, shopping carts, empty food cans, old clothing.

The camps were located under bridges and in thickets and wooded areas, not in plain sight of the trail, but nearby. One of the largest camps, covering about an acre, grew up near the 82nd Avenue commercial district. This settlement evolved into something like a village, with rules and norms for behavior.

During my time in Portland, the homeless problem became increasingly urgent. In 2015 the City Council declared a housing emergency. Like many American cities, Portland grappled with escalating housing costs and growing numbers of people living outdoors. Officials estimated there were more than four thousand homeless people in 2017. There were good homeless services for meals and some needs, but not enough beds in shelters, transitional housing, or designated campgrounds. The problem was complex and contentious. Local leaders argued about solutions.

Homeless camps were visible in many parts of town. When people complained, the police simply asked the offenders to "move along" and go somewhere else. Few relocation services existed because not enough facilities were available. The homeless got shuffled around town to appease angry citizens and businesses.

To some extent I learned to look away from the tents and scattered possessions and see them as part of the landscape. I wanted my allegiance to be with the people without homes, and I hoped to remain sensitive to their needs. But I didn't enjoy seeing the trash on the streets or the Springwater Corridor. A wonderful resource was slowly transforming into outdoor shelter for the houseless.

Many locals avoided the trail because they didn't feel safe on it. My next-door neighbor refused to walk on the Corridor without her husband along. I never worried during the day because there were so many people coming and going. The few times I walked home from the MAX using the trail at night, I felt nervous and eventually stopped going that route.

The situation heightened in 2016 when someone was stabbed at the big camp near 82nd Avenue. Reports of cyclists and pedestrians being harassed and threatened on the Corridor had increased. The usual outcry ensued. Residents and merchants complained to city hall, asking for law enforcement to do something about the homeless people taking over the trail. The police said their hands were tied by various legal protections for the homeless. Fed up with inaction, a group of business owners filed a lawsuit against the city, leading to a big sweep of the Corridor on September 1, 2016. People living near the trail fretted about the possibility of an influx of homeless people into their neighborhoods. I never noticed anyone in the streets near my house, but in other parts of Portland, sweeps merely scattered houseless people into new residential areas. A friend of mine discovered people living in a vacant house behind hers and reported it to authorities. It took several calls to get someone to board up the place. Within a week the same occupants had broken back into the house.

Following the sweep, which included a cleanup of camp debris, the Springwater Corridor looked better than ever. That I no longer saw Douglas and his long contraption at the bench near the boardwalk gave me pause. I wondered where he now parked his home on wheels. His new camp likely didn't match the serene beauty of the Corridor. A pang of remorse stabbed my chest.

ROSE CITY AUDITION

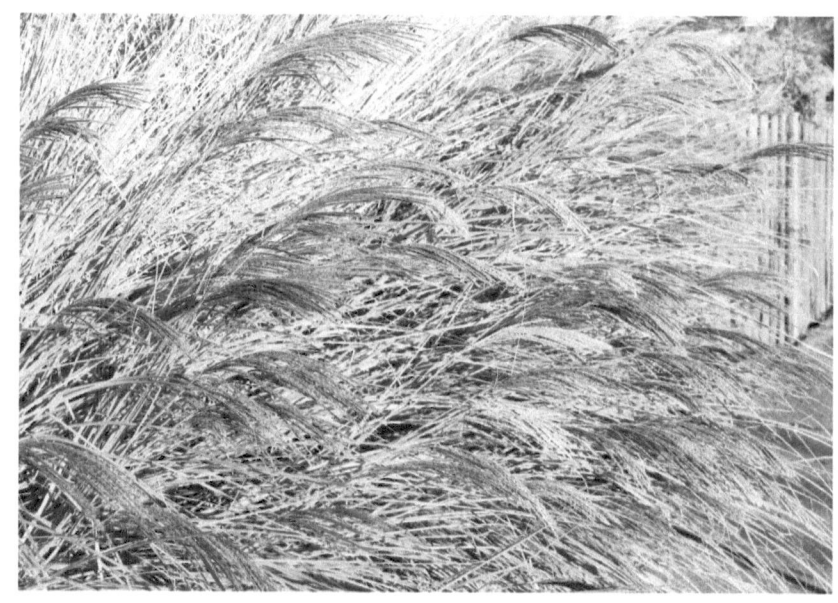

Good Hair Day

One day I take the light rail downtown to see a movie after walking a half mile to the station through snow and ice. Since I'm not meeting anyone, I don't bother to apply makeup and barely comb my hair after donning furry earmuffs. Taking a quick glance in the mirror and noting I look awful, I assure myself it doesn't matter.

As I navigate the trail from the Springwater Corridor to the MAX station, head bent and carefully stepping on the slippery surface, I hear someone call out from above.

"Hey, ma'am. I just have to tell you—you have gorgeous hair."

Startled, I glance up to see a middle-aged man in a reflective orange vest looking down at me through the trees.

"Oh . . . thank you," I reply.

"I watched you come over the ridge and was struck by how beautiful your hair is."

"That's kind of you to say. You made my day!"

The exchange is so unexpected it feels surreal. I don't think my hair is remarkable. Falling a few inches below my shoulders, it is light grey around my face and medium brown on the sides and back. The mane is thick and slightly wavy, with a few golden highlights in the sun. I suspect one reason the man noticed my locks was their contrast with the long, black wool coat I'm wearing. People seem to glance at me more when I wear that coat.

Sixty-something women rarely receive compliments on their appearance from strangers, so I bask in the glow of this unusual attention the rest of the way down. On the train ride, I reflect on what people have said about my hair at different times in my life.

As a young girl, my mother braided my blond pigtails every morning, pulling tight. I wasn't allowed to wear my hair loose, ever. In second grade, I begged to cut off the braids into a pixie style. My mother relented, only to lament bitterly when we couldn't find an Easter hat that looked good with my cropped hairdo. In high school, my long, golden blond hair received praise in the "Little Black Book" where the boys in my class wrote about the girls. On a celebratory trip to France after finishing my PhD, in my late twenties, I went to the L'Oréal Studio in Paris where student stylists offered a cheap haircut. When the instructor came around to inspect my trim, he commented, "Your hair color is beautiful." Previously, I'd never considered the color anything special.

Most of my life I've had long hair, with a few

exceptional interludes, such as the early eighties when I sported a Princess Diana style for a while. These periods didn't last long, because I always wanted to pull my hair back in hot, humid weather. My mother certainly would disapprove of my hair length, because she thought it unbecoming for older women to wear their hair long. Although most older American women have short or medium-length hair, television commercials and magazine ads for sex-enhancing products project the image of lush, flowing tresses on the older female set.

Before entering the movie theater downtown, I stop at a deli for lunch. I notice an elderly woman walking towards the counter. As a young man crosses her path, she pauses to say to him, "I really like your hair."

"Pardon?" he asks, a surprised look on his face.

"Your hair," she says, "I really like it."

He has short, jet black hair, slightly longer in the front and rakishly combed to the side. "Thank you," he replies, "I'm letting it grow out."

Does the woman's comment spur the young man to contemplate his hair, as I had mine? The symmetry of the two encounters appeals to my sense of order and harmony in the universe. Perhaps it's a special day when random people take note and compliment strangers on their locks.

I recall a recent day when I told a cashier, "You have the most beautiful blue eyes." She'd blushed and said, "You made my day." Perhaps that set in motion a ripple effect resulting in the good hair day. I'd like to think the world sometimes works that way.

Chickenmania

> *If you have a backyard and you don't keep chickens,
> many will suspect you of being a republican.*
> —Alexander Barrett,
> *This Is Portland: The City You've Heard You Should Like*[3]

Chicken keeping promised to be the glorious culmination of my Portland adventure. At last, I would achieve the pinnacle of citizenship and proudly take my place among the elite.

When my home repairs are complete in the summer of 2015, I dive into chicken raising with the zeal only a transplant can muster, anticipating great enjoyment and validation of my Portlander credentials. Finding a place with a backyard big enough to raise the large birds had figured high on my list of "must haves" when house hunting. I hadn't a clue the experience would rattle my confidence, hurtle me toward a nervous breakdown, and convert me to Buddhism.

Backyard chicken raising isn't for the meek or

insecure. Selecting a breed, designing a coop, keeping the baby chicks warm for six weeks, training the fowl to behave, protecting them from predators, letting them in and out of the run, replenishing food and water, cleaning up the poop, monitoring their health, finding chicken sitters—the demands are endless. Had I realized the complexity of the operation, I'd have blanched and reconsidered.

In one of my earliest memories, someone hoists me up to look through the glass door of an electric incubator for hatching eggs. A row of these metal contraptions line the wall in a back room of the feed store where my parents work. Inside the incubators a thermostat keeps the temperature at a steady one hundred degrees. Watching the tiny beaks crack open the eggs from the inside thrills me. Next comes a foot, a wing, a head, and the tentative, unsteady jerks of a newborn chick entering the world. When the chicks are older and soft feathers cover their bodies, I exchange pleasantries with them in the brooder, poke my fingers through the wire cage, and occasionally get to hold one.

Growing up with chickens in our backyard in rural Louisiana, I took many a turn feeding the birds and "picking" (collecting) their eggs. Even after I moved away, on visits home I made sure to still walk among the flock and check their nests, breathing in the pungent scent of straw, dusty feathers, and dried manure.

My mother never asked me to wring the necks and eviscerate the birds for the cooking pot (a messy and smelly affair), but I watched her do it many times and appreciated the exquisite dishes she prepared. Her roasted hens were celebrated by all who tasted them, and though many coveted her birds to serve guests on special occasions, only her closest friends enjoyed this privilege. Clearly, I had the bona fides to succeed as a chicken farmer, which makes it even more upsetting when I face the possibility of failure.

The author, at nine months, in her grandmother's flock

Our family's connection to chickens also has a dark, sometimes humorous side. My father became obsessed with the purchase and sale of young chickens. His work in agribusiness included brokering baby chicks on the wholesale market. He loved ordering and distributing the fowl to farm stores, where they arrived in cardboard boxes with little air holes on the side. I recall the excitement of watching the chicks' tiny heads poke through the holes as they cheeped loudly.

In mid-life, Dad was diagnosed with bipolar disorder, and he struggled for decades to keep his condition under control. Often, the first sign of a manic episode was Dad placing an order for thousands of baby chicks, more birds than could possibly be sold to his customers. His associates and my brothers had to go behind him and cancel the orders. "He's ordering chickens again," they'd report wearily, and we knew more outrageous behavior would follow. Once he covered the floor of the old Quonset hut behind the store with litter and filled the building with thousands of young chickens. The scene evoked the image of a kinetic carpet of cacophonic popcorn amid large fans blowing pungent hot air. Even after he retired and his medications were working reasonably well, Dad continued to broker baby chickens as a hobby, spending hours on the phone managing orders. "He needs this to stay sane," my mother said.

When I embark on chicken raising in Portland, the dark side of my family's chicken history doesn't enter my thinking. Only auspicious thoughts of sweet, appealing birds gracing my backyard fill my mind. The local chicken bible, *A Chicken in Every Yard: The Urban Farm Store's Guide to Chicken Keeping*,[4] by Robert and Hanna Litt, reinforces my optimism. This book provides an excellent resource, but the authors paint an overly rosy picture of the challenge at hand.

Experts often refer to chicken raising as an "art," because there are no exact rules, only rough guidelines.

What this means is you shouldn't be surprised if your chickens behave totally at odds with what you were told to expect. For example, chickens are supposed to roost at night, but mine ignore their perch and sleep on the ground or in the corner of the coop, leaving a pile of droppings in one spot. More on this topic later.

Guidebooks claim that handling chicks from a young age accustoms them to being held by humans so they grow up unafraid of people, almost like pets. Not so with my girls. Both will protest loudly if anyone comes near them, despite being gently handled daily as babies. To catch them, I have to use a dip net purchased at a sporting goods store.

"You're going to laugh when I tell you what I need this for," I told the manager.

He laughs. "Actually, you're the third person who's come in here for just that," he replied after I explain, "so it doesn't seem crazy at all."

Like a dutiful scholar, I research backyard chicken keeping extensively. In addition to the Litt bible, I pour over websites and magazine articles. I question Portlanders. By August 2015, I'm ready to begin.

The first step is to decide on a housing system for

the birds. Do I want a stationary coop and run (daytime enclosure) in which the litter has to be changed regularly, or a movable "tractor" structure that uses live grass to absorb the droppings? I prefer the latter but am unsure if my backyard provides enough lawn space to move the unit around without destroying the grass through chicken scratching. I need expert advice.

A pair of consultants from a firm I'll call Sustainable Gardens come out to advise me. Regarding the space question, they say it depends on the season, the amount of rainfall, and how much poop I can tolerate on the ground. In other words, I'll just have to try it and see. Most sources recommend giving chickens as much enclosure space as possible, affording them room to scratch and move around, so I order a four-by-eight-foot cedar tractor, a misguided choice my consultants never question. Mike, the carpenter from Sustainable Gardens, builds the unit on site, because my back gate isn't large enough to carry in a prefabricated model. Once complete, the contraption is too heavy to move around on its back wheels, so I'll have to waddle it back and forth to reposition it in a new spot. This alarms me.

Time to set up the nursery in the garage. The remote-controlled overhead door doesn't work properly and squeaks loudly when lifted by hand. Not wanting to disturb my neighbors with late night tending, I call a door repair company. They're unable to fix the automatic lift, but at least they silence the squeaking.

Tingling with nervousness and excitement, I drive to the Urban Farm Store in early August to select my chicks. The store doesn't allow ordering a particular breed so my choices are limited to what's in stock. After checking the cages for breeds that make good laying hens, I choose a brown sex-linked hybrid and a black-and-white Barred Plymouth Rock. The brown chick I name Henrietta (Henna for short), and the other one I call Pilgrim.

I take the pair home and gently place them in the brooder, a heavy plastic storage bin with heat lamp and accoutrements. Henna seems high strung and squawks about everything, especially when I remove her buddy from the bin to pet her. Pilgrim is more docile and allows me to pick her up with less fuss. The two become close pals and never leave each other's side. Even when they are older, the chickens get along fine, with only an occasional squabble.

No amount of gentle holding of the chicks calms their distress when handled. As they grow and become more rambunctious, I give up on having a cuddly relationship with them. Any intrusion into the brooder, such as replenishing its floor with clean pine chips, sparks loud protests.

Feeding and watering the flock isn't a problem, but I fret about keeping the temperature right. For the

first two weeks, the brooder should be kept between ninety-five and one hundred degrees; then, over the next few weeks, the temperature should be reduced by five degrees each week until the birds begin to grow feathers. I check the thermometer several times a day, sometimes wondering if the gauge might be inaccurate. When we have a triple-digit hot spell in late August, I worry the chicks will overheat in the sweltering garage.

Tension and worry over the birds begin to take their toll. I have trouble sleeping. I find myself looking in on the flock more often than needed, just for reassurance. I fear my neighbors will notice my obsession and feel pity. Will I botch my audition to become a Portlander over a pair of silly birds?

As the weeks go by and the time to transfer the chicks to the coop looms closer, I dread the move. Will they adapt to their new home or find ways to revolt? I anguish over the possibility the cedar enclosure might emit strong vapors that could damage the young birds' delicate lungs. The possibility of catastrophe seems to hover ominously.

Right on schedule, at eight weeks, I move the flock into the coop. I keep them inside for a week before opening the door to the run, to give the birds time to adjust to their new home. At first they hang back, occasionally peeking out the door, then quickly retreat to safety. After about an hour, Pilgrim summons the courage to saunter down the stair-step to the ground, followed tentatively by Henna. Once in the run, the fowl enthusiastically scratch for bugs.

I hope the chicks will find their way back into the coop at dusk, but they don't. The birds sleep in a corner of the run the first few nights. The books mention this possibility and advise carrying the chickens into the coop at night until they get the hang of it. The design of the run doesn't allow me to reach its far corners, so I use the dip net. You'd swear I am brutally dismembering the animals the way they squawk bloody murder. Releasing them inside the coop evokes equal trauma, as their claws tangle with the mesh. After a couple of nights of this, I give up. "Go ahead and sleep on the ground," I scoff. "See if I care."

But I do care. Will predators dig under the run at night? I search online forums for ideas on enticing chickens into their coop. One blog recommends turning on a light in the coop so it's brighter inside than out, signaling that inside is "home." Really? I don't recall reading anything about having to illuminate the coop to get chickens to come in at night. Apparently, poultry requires a great deal of coaxing to behave properly.

Though skeptical, I hang a flashlight inside the coop, turn it on at dusk, and watch expectantly from my office window. It works! Henna and Pilgrim climb up the stairs and enter the coop. After a while, I go out to close the coop door and turn off the light.

After performing the light routine for three nights, I try not doing it. Will the birds sleep on the perch or retire inside? My entire body tenses with anticipation as I watch from the window.

They don't enter the coop. Cursing, I resign myself to a permanent role as lightkeeper. But the next night, lo and behold, Henna and Pilgrim retreat into the coop twenty-five minutes before dusk. Stunned and elated, I give thanks that something is finally going my way. And they continue to do it the next night and the next. They are trained—hallelujah!

Henna always leads the way into the coop at dusk, but she has to cajole Pilgrim into coming along. Thrilled by this new achievement, I revel in watching the girls enter their bedroom each evening. With the shade up and lights off, I settle in before dusk to watch the show. First, the birds preen on the roost in the run, then they take one or two tentative forays into the coop before finally retreating inside. The thought of them all cozy in their coop gives me a warm feeling, and for the first time, I can relax.

Soon, new worries arise—the flock might destroy every inch of grass in the backyard and I'll be left with bare earth splattered with chicken shit.

The time has come to move the unit to a fresh spot. How often I need to do this to avoid killing the grass remains unknown. Sources recommend everything from several times a day to every few days. I attempt the first move after five days.

Having learned the hard way that a four-by-eight tractor is too large for a moveable unit, I nevertheless manage to wobble the structure from side to side, little by little positioning it over a different patch of lawn.

After each move, I level the front end with pavers to accommodate the slope in my yard. This creates gaps between tufts of grass, spaces that need plugging to keep out predators. The possibility nighttime critters might slink in and kill my charges terrifies me. During the day, stray cats stare hungrily from a distance.

The lawn isn't in great shape to begin with because of the summer drought, so keeping two chickens penned inside a thirty-two-square-foot area does noticeable damage. To encourage the grass to regrow, I

water the affected area, along with the rest of the yard to help its recovery from the drought. By moving the house every five days, I will cover about half the yard space in a month. After that, the flock will be old enough, at twelve weeks, to saunter out and forage during the day, so they'll do less damage inside the run.

Watching the birds grow into healthy young hens, scratching for bugs, complacently roosting in their run, or sweetly nestled together in the coop, elates me. I love listening to their jovial chatter during the day, and the trilling calls at dusk, signaling time to turn in for the night.

Nevertheless, the stress of the operation continues to wear me down. Uneasy feelings wash over me several times a day. For the first time in years, I feel the need to pray often.

More problems with the coop heighten my anxiety. Rainwater backtracks under the roof, soaking the chicks and their bedding. Mike has to come and raise the pitch of the roof and attach a tarp over the rear air vent. Additionally, the birds refuse to roost on the bar in the coop. Instead, they sleep in a corner, making it necessary for me to scoop out the soiled litter each morning so the birds don't sleep in the previous night's waste. Once when that happened, the chickens came out with feces stuck to their feet—an alarming sight.

More and more, I wonder if perhaps I'm not cut out for chicken raising, after all. My thoughts turn bleak as I contemplate my predicament.

Around this time, I discover that listening to Gregorian chants online provides soothing comfort for my anxiety. I bookmark my favorite chant sites and add this to my prayer routine.

At twelve weeks, I let the chickens out into the yard. Will they return to the coop at dusk, or will I have to chase them around the yard with a dip net?

To my great relief, the chicks return to their house at dusk every night. Had they stayed outdoors, I'd have let them fend for themselves, predators be damned.

The chicken house becomes stationary after I realize the grass doesn't grow enough in winter to recover from the birds' scratching. I'll need straw to litter the run. The man at the farm store loads the tightly packed bale into my car. Because the bundle weighs more than I can lift, I back the car up the driveway to the garage entrance and roll it out. But I waffle about cutting the ties, not knowing if the straw will spring out in all directions. Also, will I need to crawl into the feces-splattered run to spread the straw evenly?

It rains a few days, providing an excuse to procrastinate. My anxiety grows. At last, I snip the ties. Voila! The bundle stays compacted. I peel off small sections at a time and carry them to the coop. I spread the straw with a short rake without entering the run. Satisfaction at being chicken competent floods my being. I have a fully functional chicken house and can breathe a little easier.

I'm not sure why I worry so much about every aspect of the chicken operation. Each week seems to bring on a new crisis. When I change the birds' feed at twelve weeks, as recommended, at first, they go on a hunger strike and I fear they'll never eat again.

My son Graham asks, "Have you talked to your therapist about this?" I don't have a therapist at the moment, but his question prompts me to find one.

Marcia is sympathetic and astute. She helps me figure out that the chickens strained my coping resources following two years of intense adaptation to a new city, all the while undertaking one home improvement after another. Raising the flock also brought back anxieties I'd experienced as a single mother raising two sons without family support. I remind myself that my birds are not babies, the world won't end if something bad happens to them, and I can get rid of them any time. More than one friend counsels me to find homes for the chickens immediately, but after all I've invested, I can't give up yet.

Marcia suggests I try mindfulness meditation. For years, I've scoffed at the proliferation of mindful approaches to every aspect of life, convinced the practice offered little pragmatic benefit. Nevertheless, willing to try anything, I start a daily meditation practice, beginning with online videos and library books to get me going. I set a large cushion on a rug in my bedroom and each afternoon I sit lotus-style and try to clear my mind. Using beginner's tricks, I slowly count backwards from one hundred, imagine clouds drifting across a blue sky, or focus on my breath moving in and out. To my surprise, I find noticeable relief from my worries. In time, meditation will lead me to study Buddhism and join a local sangha of practitioners, an outcome I will cherish with gratitude. In the meantime, however, my chicken travails continue to burden my psyche.

Will I ever get used to the intimate contact with poop that chicken keeping requires? Apparently, the birds are never going to use the low roost in the coop. Having put a cardboard liner in their sleeping corner to protect the floor, each morning I remove the night's droppings and spread fresh litter. The other contact with excrement comes from my deck, which gets its share of turds as the chickens roam the yard. The waste washes off easily with a garden hose, but I have to watch my step going out the back door.

Speaking of poop, one day I find myself going out to the chicken house, flashlight in hand and raincoat protecting me from the drizzle, to shine a light on the chickens' hindquarters. I check for signs of "pasting," a condition where feces crust over the anus and form a protruding plug that can cause serious problems. Visual inspection reveals nothing, although the books say one needs to move the tail feathers aside to get a good look, something I haven't the courage to try.

For all my fear of predators, I observe only one instance where the flock seems in danger. A loud ruckus in the backyard sets my heart pounding as I hurry to the window. A large grey hawk swooshes down and lands on the edge of the garage, gazing intently at the birds. Henna squawks and flaps her wings. Pilgrim scurries into the hedge. The hawk soon takes off and I breathe a sigh of relief. Another time, a black-and-white cat hides behind the chicken house, keeping a watchful eye on the grazing fowl. I think he plans to attack, but he quickly skirts around the chickens to exit the yard.

The girls and I settle into a daily routine. I let them out into the yard around eight in the morning, check food and water, and remove droppings. Even this five-minute task feels burdensome. In the afternoons, the curious pullets peck on the glass doors to my bedroom, interrupting my siesta. I try to convince myself this soft tapping sounds companionable, but in fact it feels vaguely menacing.

To remind myself of my original intent, I take a few moments each day to enjoy watching Henna and

Pilgrim forage. Scratch, scratch. Peck, peck, peck. Sometimes they sit on the roost, gazing out placidly. In the morning and afternoon, when the sun shines through the run, the girls bask in the light illuminating their beautiful plumage. In the evening, I still watch the retreat into the coop performance, complete with Pilgrim's last-minute forays outside before retiring. Then I go out to close the door to the run. It gives me pleasure to know the chicks are secure for the night, protected from predators.

Still, my enjoyment of the flock fails to outweigh the caretaking burden and mental strain. During my Thanksgiving visit with my son in Seattle, I worry that the teenage chicken sitter I've hired will forget to close the coop after dark and I'll come home to dead birds.

By the end of November, teetering on a nervous breakdown, I reluctantly accept my failure as a chicken farmer. I'll keep the fowl through the holidays so my sons can see them during their visit. Afterward, I'll find a new home for Henna and Pilgrim. Making the decision brings enough relief to get me through the first weeks of December.

There must be a profound lesson to be learned from this chicken-raising experience, I think. But I remain too close to figure it out.

On December 28th I place an ad on Craigslist:

Free Chickens: two chickens almost 5 months old, soon

to start laying. One Barred Plymouth Rock, one Brown Sex-linked. Both healthy and well cared-for, but I can't keep them.

Within minutes I receive replies. I contact the first respondent, Dimitri, immediately, and smile to myself when he says he'll come right away to pick up the birds.

"How are you going to transport the chickens?" I ask. "Should I get some rope to tie their legs together?" That's what my mother did when moving live chickens.

"Oh, no," Dimitri replies, clearly alarmed by this idea. "It might hurt them. I'll bring a box to put them in."

"That's good," I say meekly, embarrassed I suggested something that might hurt the animals.

As luck would have it, Henna and Pilgrim rest inside the run, so I close the door to keep them where we can catch them. We'll need to use the dip net. Will Dimitri consider that cruel as well?

I vigorously clean house, trying to contain my excitement. All I can think about is how I'll soon be rid of my charges. Henna and Pilgrim are going to a good home, with a one-acre pasture in which to graze.

Dimitri arrives with his wife, teenage son, and a small cardboard box. The son, I learn, loves animals and will care for the chicks.

"You have a coop?" I ask.

"Yes, it's similar to yours but a bit different. And the chickens, are they in good health?"

I answer affirmatively.

Dimitri hesitates to use the dip net. Eventually, he takes it from me and carefully catches the birds, who remain surprisingly calm. Into the box they go, and the family leaves with their free fowl. So focused on divesting myself of this burden, I forget completely about offering the new owners the leftover food and accessories.

Am I truly free of the chickens? Within two hours of placing an ad? Wow. The relief is almost palpable.

Barely time to celebrate. I have to take the light rail downtown for a movie. Riding the train north, I try to calm down and enjoy the first snowflakes of winter. But a disturbing thought intrudes. *I didn't mention anything about the chickens not using the roost to sleep. Shit. They may do the same at the new place. What if Dimitri calls to ask why the birds are sleeping on the floor? What if he wants to return them because of this?* My anxiety skyrockets.

Even the riveting acting in *The Danish Girl* can't impede worrisome thoughts about the chickens and their aberrant sleeping habits. I failed to disclose that my chickens had "special needs." *Why didn't I?* It wasn't an intentional omission; I simply had not given any thought to the matter as I contemplated giving the flock away. How could I have forgotten one of the biggest sources of my distress?

When I return home, the message light blinks ominously. *Oh, no.* Indeed, I recognize Dimitri's accent immediately on the recording.

"Can you please give me a call? I have a couple of questions about the chickens."

Holy shit, I'm done for now, I think. Then I notice the message was left at 3:34 p.m., before the chicks' bedtime. Maybe the call didn't concern their sleeping habits after all. Still, with trepidation, I return the call. No one answers so I leave a message.

Will Dimitri phone the next day and accuse me of withholding information? I'd assured him the pullets were healthy, but did that include behavioral abnormalities? Am I guilty of fraud?

I figure if they are going to call it might not be until evening, after work. In preparation, I rehearse the explanation I'll give to cover my ass.

The chickens are sleeping on the floor? Oh, it might take them a while to start using the roost. When I first moved them into the coop, they didn't use the roost at all, but over time they began using it occasionally, and now one uses it regularly (true) *and the other one some of the time* (an exaggeration). *Also, I read that some chickens don't begin to roost consistently until they begin laying eggs* (true).

What if they ask to return the chickens?

I'm sorry, but I have health problems and I'm unable to care for them (true). *Also, I will be going out of town soon so won't be here to tend to them* (an exaggeration).

So why didn't you tell us about the sleeping problem up front?

I was so nervous about the whole transfer thing I didn't

think of it. I meant to offer you some chicken supplies too but forgot.

Several days pass without a call. I begin to relax and enjoy the freedom from animal care. *Am I truly off the hook for these blasted birds?* Apparently so. After nearly six months of sustained anxiety over chicken raising, I can reclaim a measure of peace.

The next morning, I hose semi-frozen poop off the deck for the last time.

In early spring, I sell the chicken house for a fraction of its cost and throw in the accessories for free. Removing the remnants of chickenmania more than compensates for the financial loss.

In the end, I come to view my chicken ordeal as a unique kind of suffering, one which led me to Buddhism and a more insightful approach to life. After years of searching, I had found my spiritual home. Something worth so much more than proving my Portlander credentials.

ROSE CITY AUDITION

A Reluctant Rosarian

When I told people I'd inherited thirty-five rosebushes with my Portland house, most congratulated me on my good fortune, while a few offered sympathy. My own feelings were ambivalent. Like many aspects of my Portland life, having a personal rose garden conferred blessings and burdens. The plentiful blooms were gorgeous and a source of pride, but caretaking was demanding and stressful. I wanted to succeed not only to enjoy the fruits of my labor; becoming an accomplished rosarian would bolster my status as an authentic Portlander. Having failed at chicken keeping, surely I could succeed at growing roses.

Rosebushes are about as common as rhododendrons and camellias in Portland, but to plant thirty-five bushes struck me as excessive, even for an enthusiast. Both the previous owner Michael of the sparkly eyes, and the owner before him, loved roses. Some of the bushes may even predate those owners, judging by the thickness of their trunks and branches. A landscaper once commented, "That's some wood you got on those roses." In the backyard, the trunk of an ancient climbing rose stood seven feet tall, its thick, new canes shooting straight up to the sky, their tips reaching fifteen feet. In time, these canes would bend over, and I could tie them to a trellis, but while sticking straight up the branches frightened me.

My garden boasted every size, shape, and color of roses. I couldn't name any of them, but I had my favorites. I loved the large blooms with thickly packed, velvety petals. Those with flimsy petals seemed like second-class citizens. My color preferences were deep red and yellow; pink and purple were boring. Fragrance didn't matter much because my nose was sensitive to only a few varieties.

The placement of the rosebushes in my yard seemed random, except for those lining the sidewalk to the front steps. One oddly shaped plant looked ridiculous sitting alone next to a birch tree in the strip between the sidewalk and the street. I moved it to one of the beds closer to the house. In the backyard, several rosebushes were planted along the perimeter of the overgrown hedge. When the hedge was cut back, the bushes looked forlorn and out of place. I transplanted about a third of the rosebushes throughout the yard, grouping them into clusters of similar size bushes. That's when I came to appreciate the hardiness of these plants. Not only do roses transplant easily, but the vestiges of roots left behind often regenerate.

I knew a little about growing roses from having

planted a bunch in my Tampa yard. In that environment the big menace was root damage from nematodes. Picking the right rootstock resistant to pests was key to success. I'd planted about a dozen low-growing Floribunda plants, which came in a profusion of colors and scents. Following the recommendations of the specialty shop where I bought the plants, I used a three-in-one systemic fertilizer, pesticide, and fungicide, and never had any problems with black spot. I'd dutifully deadheaded the blooms and enjoyed months of lovely flowering. Contrary to popular assumptions, rose growing seemed to be easier than widely believed.

My success with Florida rose husbandry gave me hope I could manage the bushes thrust under my care in Portland. I felt honored to receive this living gift, a precious gem worthy of loving stewardship. I fed, watered, and pruned the bushes regularly. During the dry summer months, I intertwined a drip hose around the plant bases. After every blooming flush, I clipped off the spent flowers. But the one thing that caught me unprepared was the menace of black spot. This fungal disease attacks the leaves unmercifully, causing them to wither and drop, sometimes killing the plant. In a city with as much rain as Portland, fighting black spot takes heroic effort.

At first, I treated the fungus with natural remedies such as homemade solutions of water, soap, and baking soda. I assumed use of chemical fungicides was taboo in the Rose City's ecofriendly culture. Despite spraying weekly, the organic spray failed to control the spread of disease, and more and more leaves acquired dark round spots, turned yellow, and fell. Online research steered me away from combination products, dismissing them as ineffective for disease prevention. Websites recommended a heavy-duty fungicide.

On spraying days, I donned long sleeves and pants to protect my skin from the harsh chemicals that inevitably blew back on my body. To do a good job, one must spray the undersides of leaves as well as the tops, along with the canes and the ground below. This required a lot of bending and stretching. Moreover, to reach all the leaves required getting close to the bush, with its thorns that ripped my clothing and drew blood across my skin. Completing the spraying task took over an hour, followed by exhaustion and the icky feeling of being soaked in carcinogens. The process had to be repeated every ten days or so throughout the blooming season. On spraying days, I worried that my next-door neighbor, whose yard sat only a few feet away and got misted, would disapprove of my fungicide use.

Spraying for black spot ranked first among my least favored Portland activities. Onerous, tedious, constant, discouraging, and toxic. I read about a local woman who got fed up with the whole routine and removed all her rosebushes. I admired her courage.

Insects weren't a problem (for the plants, at least—

spiders love rosebushes, and I'm arachnophobic). But one rose malady stumped even the experts. The problem appeared on an older bush that produced large, exquisite blooms of the deepest hue. Buds couldn't open properly because of the hardened outer layer. This damaged, darkened crust showed no signs of insects or other pathogens. The leaves and branches on the bush appeared vigorous and healthy. Once the bloom broke through the encasement, the inside petals appeared normal.

I wanted to save this beautiful but sickly bush. The first expert to examine it was the consultant from Sustainable Gardens whom I'd hired to build the chicken coop. She couldn't identify the problem but speculated that it might be a virus. Then she asked, "What do you use to control black spot?" *Busted*, I thought. Sheepishly, I named the product that dominates the market.

"You can go ahead and use up the rest of your bottle, because I know it's expensive. But please don't continue to use this harmful chemical. It's bad for the environment and there are safer alternatives available."

Easy for you to say, I thought. Still, guilt gnawed at me for violating local norms of gardening propriety. For a while I tried copper-based fungicide but eventually returned to the hard stuff. Didn't my mental health take priority? Maybe in time I would find a way to go organic.

My next step was to show the malady to a guy

working the information desk at Portland Nursery. After carefully examining the petals, he put the shell under a microscope, but no pathology was evident. He consulted reference books and gathered staff for opinions. No one had seen this problem before. Since the disease might spread to nearby plants, he advised removal of the sick bush. Regretfully, I dug up the plant. That act sparked the next phase of my rose husbandry—thinning out the bushes to a more manageable number.

Having fewer plants would lighten my workload and provide the added benefit of increased air circulation between bushes, which reduces the spread of fungal spores. I began by removing the smaller bushes surrounding the backyard patio. After taking a long, hard look at the climbing rose, I decided it had to go. I couldn't hack climbing on ladders to tether the unwieldy canes. When the time came for the annual shrubbery pruning, I instructed my landscaper to cut down the climbing rose. "Are you sure?" he asked, "This one's so old and beautiful." With a pang of guilt, I said, "Yes, take it down. It's unmanageable."

In anticipation of removing the climbing rose, I memorialized its lovely pink blossoms in a short video posted on YouTube. This required setting up a channel and learning some basic editing tricks so I could upload the video. In the clip, the blossoms are at the peak of their beauty, abundant and swaying softly in the wind. Against a deep blue sky, the delicate pink flowers evoke warm sensations. I named the video "Pink Climbing Rose," and, to my surprise, it got hundreds of views.

A large stump remained above the ground after the landscaper cut down the climbing rose. Three times new shoots emerged from its gnarled carcass, and each time I sprayed herbicide to kill them. The shoots withered but the plant refused to die. The next time the shoots appeared, I surrendered. "OK, you win. Grow."

In the front yard, I targeted the bushes with flimsy petals and least favorite colors. These I photographed and posted as Free Stuff on Craigslist. A woman came and dug them up, not an easy task because rosebushes have deep, strong roots.

Thinning complete, my rose garden consisted of a dozen specimens, mostly red, with one yellow and one lavender bicolored bloom. The remaining bushes I tended with care and they produced a plethora of flowers. During the 2017 season, my last one in Portland, the blooms appeared in April and continued nonstop into December. Passersby stopped to admire the flowers and compliment my work. The little girl next door took a fancy to the flowers and came over to smell them. When I noticed a particularly beautiful rose, I sometimes put it in water and left it on her doorstep.

Despite having better air circulation, the bushes still suffered from black spot. I continued to spray regularly during the growing season, but with only a third the number of bushes, the burden had lightened.

During that final season I received so many compliments about the roses that it went to my head. I decided to enter the biggest competition of the year, the Portland Spring Rose Show. I had attended two previous shows where I took photos of the prize-winning entries. On those visits I assumed one had to be a member of the Portland Rose Society to enter the contest, but someone later told me that wasn't necessary. Furthermore, my informant assured me, not knowing the kind of roses one grew wasn't disqualifying. People at the show would help to identify the kind of rose and determine the category in which it belonged. I met the eligibility criteria to enter my roses!

I read detailed instructions on the show's website, including a helpful page on "Pointers for Novice and First-Time Rose Exhibitors."[5] Cut several candidate roses the night before and put them in water. Look for blooms a little more than halfway open, although fully open roses are acceptable. The next morning, choose the most beautiful of the lot for the show. Don't remove any leaves until after arriving at the venue and it's time to put the flower in a vase provided by the organizers. Make sure not to cut the stem too short, a mistake often made by novices.

My roses looked most stunning in their partially open form, so I set my sights on entering that group.

Timing was critical, because the only specimens I would have to work with were blooms that happened to be at the right stage on the day of the contest, June 8th. In the week leading up to the show, I anxiously surveyed all of my roses, trying to gauge which ones might be ripe for picking June 7th. The prospects weren't encouraging. A few buds were beginning to open, but they needed more time. Others looked good but were likely to be past their prime in a few days. Surely, after all my work and planning, I would have at least one suitable entry on the big day.

Not a single rose in my garden met the minimum criteria for entry. Only new buds and spent blooms could be found.

Gratefully, missing my only shot at the contest didn't upset me, something I credited to two years of daily meditation focused on accepting things as they are. I continued to lovingly tend and appreciate my roses. The joy they brought to me and the neighborhood revealed their true glory.

Sesame Salmon Baked in Foil

Growing up in Louisiana, the only salmon my mother prepared was a Creole dish made with canned salmon and tomato sauce, served over rice. In Portland, for the first time I had abundant access to fresh salmon and learned new recipes. A real Portlander should be able to prepare a mean salmon dish. To that end, I experimented with different methods of preparation and seasoning. I wanted to develop my own special recipe that would wow guests. I set my sights on creating the perfect salmon baked in foil. Through trial and error, I developed this prize-worthy, Asian-influenced recipe.

2 salmon fillets
2 tsp. olive oil
2 tsp. toasted sesame seed oil
sesame seeds
green onion tops
soy sauce
sliced lemon
salt & pepper
heavy-duty aluminum foil

Cut two rectangles of foil large enough to wrap around the fillets. Place fish on foil, skin side down. Mix oils in a small dish and brush on top and sides of fillets. Sprinkle sesame seeds, salt, and pepper on fillets. Splash a few dollops of soy sauce on the fillets, cover with lemon slices, and drape a length of green onion on top. Fold over sides of foil and crimp closed to keep juices inside.

Place fillets on a baking sheet and bake at 400° for 15 minutes. Check for doneness and continue cooking 5 minutes if needed. Remove lemon slices and onion from fillets (optional) and serve in foil on plates.

Two Minutes of Totality

*A solar eclipse, sympathetic joy,
and the rocky terrain of friendship*

As far as the eye can see, campers, cars, tents, folding chairs, canopies, and bright blue portable toilets cover the landscape adjoining the Municipal Airport of Madras, a small town in central Oregon. A man waves us to the next vacant plot under a scorching sun, a twenty-by-twenty-foot square in an open field. Dry grass stubble dots the sunbaked earth where we unfurl my new three-person tent, home for one night as we await with great anticipation the next morning's solar eclipse.

Knowing my companion Ralph will have a preference for which direction the tent faces, because everything in his orbit must be arranged just so, I ask him where we should position the door. He looks seriously in each direction. Unable to decide, he turns to our neighbor and asks for his opinion. "Man, I don't know," the young dude replies, "I'm gonna sleep in my car."

Seeing that this decision could mushroom into a Camp David deliberation, I swiftly declare, "We'll face the morning sun where the eclipse will appear."

The straw-colored bunchgrass in our field has been mowed recently and looks innocuous enough as we stake the tent floor into the surrounding dirt. I make the mistake of using my foot to hammer a stake into the hard earth, bending the thin metal out of shape.

"Don't step on the stakes to push them in," I caution Ralph. "I just tried it and bent a stake."

A few minutes later, I see Ralph pressing down on a stake with his foot.

"You're doing exactly what I just told you not to," I say, incredulously.

"I can gauge the pressure of my foot," he retorts. "I know when to ease up. If I damage one of your stakes, I'll find an exact replica on the internet and order a replacement."

Floor staked, we move on to inserting the cross poles into their sleeves. That goes fine, but the poles won't fit into the rings attached to the corners of the tent floor. After checking the instructions, I realize we should have raised the cross poles *before* staking down the tent. When I note this, Ralph seems to lose confidence in my grasp of the problem, looks around and asks, "Is there someone who knows about erecting tents?"

"We don't need to ask anyone for help, Ralph," I reassure him. "We can simply pull up the stakes and start over." To bolster my case, I add, "I read it in the directions."

Ralph surveys the neighboring campers, presumably to assess their utility. I mentally fasten my seatbelt and prepare for turbulence.

Ralph and I had met through mutual friends in the Quaker Meeting of Tampa almost twenty years beforehand, during a period when I explored different faiths. A burly, balding Midwesterner, periodically Ralph came into town and looked me up, and we'd enjoy long-winded discussions of world religions. A mathematician by training, Ralph lived in a world of numbers and precision. He often asked me to tell him the exact measure of things: What is the temperature in Portland today? How many miles is Mt. Jefferson from Mt. Hood? How many inches of rainfall do you get annually?

I used to respond truthfully— "I don't know. I'd have to check." Over time, I tired of repeated failures to respond to his queries and began to make up answers. For example, I'd take a wild guess about the temperature. "It's 62 degrees," I'd say with utmost conviction, and the certitude of presenting a numeral seemed to satisfy him.

The 2017 solar eclipse first caught my attention in February, before all the fanfare erupted in Oregon and the rest of the country. It sounded like something worth checking out—the first total eclipse visible from the U.S. since 1979.

It was an event of a lifetime! Moreover, the zone of totality would privilege Oregon as the first state to go dark for a few precious minutes as the moon aligned perfectly between the Earth and the sun.

Sometime in the spring, I look at an online map and note that the quaint town of McMinnville falls within Oregon's eclipse path. Only forty miles southwest of Portland, the town can be reached via one of the smaller highways likely to have less traffic than the interstates. This historic village ranked high on my list of interesting destinations for a day trip.

Meanwhile, I begin making plans to take a series of short trips to Eastern Oregon for my summer vacation—the Sisters Outdoor Quilt Show, Smith Rock, Hells Canyon, Baker City. I'll complete my travels with a trip to McMinnville.

When I mention the eclipse to Ralph in late spring, he has not heard much about it but sounds interested. He lives on the East Coast above the path of totality, so he'll need to travel to see the full eclipse. "You're welcome to come to Oregon," I offer, and he says he'll think about it. From past experience, I know Ralph will put off as long as possible making a decision. Meanwhile, I go ahead with my vacation plans.

In between my trips to Eastern Oregon, Ralph's

focus on the eclipse seems to sharpen and he begins talking about coming to Oregon. I mention that I plan to attend the Garrison Keillor concert a few days before the eclipse and need to purchase my ticket. Will he need a ticket as well?

The next morning, I find a Travelocity itinerary in my Inbox, confirming Ralph's nonrefundable flight plans to spend nine days with me for the eclipse . . . NINE DAYS!

Determined to take the high road, I respond with measured restraint and only slight sarcasm:

"The dates of your visit will work, but next time please check with me before making flight arrangements. You never know when there might be a conflict if you do not inform your host of the dates you will be staying with them."

Predictably, the sarcasm escapes him (or so he pretends).

"Thanks, will do - next time! It was almost 1:30 AM EST when I was getting some reasonable search results; and I decided to act immediately! Looking forward to trip!"

The prospect of spending nine days continuously in Ralph's company, or anyone's, for that matter, knots my stomach. My need for solitude is inescapable. I ponder how I'll cope with the strain of constant companionship. Keeping a lid on my irritability will be the biggest challenge. Ralph's visit will require exceptional discipline, and I'll need to prepare myself rigorously.

The centerpiece of my coping plan will be a focused cultivation of *mudita*, or sympathetic joy, the Buddhist practice of taking delight in the good fortune of others. I'd studied the concept in a meditation class earlier in the year and welcomed the opportunity to practice it for a good cause. I will put Ralph's desires first and take pleasure in helping him experience a blissful eclipse. After all, he was one of only two friends who visited me during five years living in Portland. That counts for a lot in my book. Moreover, it never occurs to me that I might justifiably refuse to host him for that many days. I'll make the best of my predicament.

With the tent set up, it's time to lay out the sleeping bags. I remember with pleasure finding a great bag for Ralph at the Goodwill Outlet Store near my house, where goods are sold by the pound. The thick gold rollup plus a new foam pad will nicely cushion the bumpy ground. I hand these items to Ralph to unroll inside the tent.

"Oh my God!" Ralph cries out.

Alarmed, I look inside and find Ralph staring anxiously at a ten-inch spike of bunchgrass poking through the tent floor *and* the foam sleeping pad. The dried blade is sharp as an ice pick.

"Holy shit," I mutter. *We should have tamped down the grass before laying out the tent.* We feel around the floor for other dangers. Days later, at an Oregon Trail museum, we'll marvel over vivid accounts of wagon oxen injured by these sharp grasses.

An hour later, we sit exhausted in our matching camp chairs, one red, one blue. Ralph hasn't asked if I already owned all the gear or had to buy things for the outing. Of the many things I bought, including the red chair for Ralph, I'd only mentioned the butane stove, noting it was a type I hadn't used before, so I was a bit nervous about figuring it out.

Time to fix dinner. Reluctantly, I begin reading the instructions for operating the stove. I chuckle to myself as I read the safety warnings we've already violated.

"Oh my, we've already broken some rules here. We put the fuel canister near a flammable object, the extra can of gas," I say, with mock concern.

Impervious to humor under stress, Ralph intones, "We'll arrange the car differently next time."

I begin assembling the stove, consulting the instructions as I go, worrying I might cause an explosion.

"Are you planning on using that stove here?" Ralph asks.

"Would I be reading these instructions if I wasn't going to use the stove, Ralph?"

Fuck mudita.

"And why do you always ask such ridiculous, obvious questions, anyway?" I harangue.

"Because I am a mathematician!" Ralph booms,

abruptly standing and flinging open the tent flap. "I ask questions to verify things. There's nothing wrong with verification . . . and I'm going inside."

I raise my voice to be heard inside the tent: "You're not a mathematician any longer. You're retired and should act like a normal person."

"It's my nature to be precise. Some people like you may not like it, but that's my nature."

"It might be your nature, but you come across as a real *nerd*," I say scornfully.

"You act like a nerd, too!" Ralph retorts.

"Yes, I'm a nerd, but at least I know I'm a nerd and I want to be told when I act nerdy."

After a pause, I ask haughtily, "If you're such a precise mathematician, why don't you help me figure out this damn stove?"

Silence.

Within a minute, a neighbor approaches, not the man sleeping in his car but the male half of an older couple sedately surveying the encampment. I'd chatted briefly with the two earlier and noted their well-equipped campsite. "I see you have the newer model of the stove I keep on my boat. Maybe I can help out here."

"Oh, what a kind angel you are," I coo, wondering how many other people observed my spat with Ralph. I hope we didn't look like a bickering old couple. A pair of misfits, fine, or simply stressed out pilgrims like the rest of the campers, even better.

We get the stove lit and I heat up the black beans I'd cooked for Ralph's arrival in Portland that never got eaten. A while later, Ralph emerges from the tent refreshed, calm, hungry. Our tempers cooled, we enjoy a hot meal under the stars of the Oregon High Desert and reminisce about old times.

In only a few hours we'll experience the spectacle of the total eclipse, that moment of surreal darkness when the sun's corona shines brilliantly in the sky. A quiet reverence pervades the camp. People speak in hushed tones; there is no music. A sense of spiritual anticipation hangs in the air.

About two weeks before the eclipse, Ralph's attention to our plans intensifies. He begins studying the many websites with information about the path of totality, eclipse duration, traffic predictions, and weather advisories. He sends me a map of Oregon showing the path and center line of the eclipse across the state and instructs: "Check weather forecast. Work out route to one of these towns."

Aha! I'm ahead of you, Ralph, I think, and send him a detailed message about McMinnville, the planned festivities at its space museum, the town's historic charm, and a link to the Google maps route from Portland.

He replies: "Duration of totality in McMinnville is only 55 sec; in Dallas 1 m 57 sec. We should go to a place with longer totality."

I pause to remind myself: *Mudita* . . . *Mudita* . . . *Mudita*

After several deep breaths, I write: "To me, one or two minutes doesn't make that much difference. Just remember I previously wrote to you on July 7th that I was making plans to go to McMinnville. Feel free to find a different location, but I don't feel like investing more effort in it. I will go wherever you prefer, provided the route is not too congested." Since I'd be doing all the driving (Ralph had a leg problem), I hoped to avoid getting stuck in sweltering traffic. Temperatures were predicted to be in the upper 90s.

A flurry of emails and phone calls works out the details of a complex plan to watch the eclipse from Madras, dubbed the "epicenter" of the state's totality zone. Authorities predict the town's population of six thousand will swell to a hundred thousand for the event. Hotels and campgrounds have sold out weeks in advance, and every day the media report ever-more-dire predictions about total gridlock on all roads leading there. Travelers headed to one of the hot spots are advised to leave two days in advance; otherwise, they could get stuck in bumper-to-bumper traffic on August 21st.

Fears about road congestion lead to hotel cancellations, and the Madras Airport opens up more fields for camping. These developments allow our final plan to unfold. We'll leave for Madras two days early, stay in a local Econolodge one night, camp at the airport the night before the eclipse, and stay at another Econolodge in nearby Prineville the following night. Ralph will pick up the tab for the hotels, which have jacked up their rates for the big event.

I take charge of planning the travel route, assembling the camping gear, planning meals and snacks for the road, and shopping for groceries and supplies. At one point Ralph suggests we add to our schedule a side trip to an old growth forest. I give him the task of finding a forest to visit, fitting it into our itinerary, and mapping out the route. I don't expect him to follow through with the task, but by assigning it to him, I relinquish responsibility. Later, when I ask how he's coming along with the search, he punts, explaining that "during our excursions, if an old growth is nearby, we can visit, time permitting. Otherwise, I wouldn't go out of my way for it - it seems we have so much on our plate already!!"

It feels like most of the stuff is on *my* plate, not *ours*. But then, I'm the one who made a solemn vow to practice sympathetic joy throughout this experience, not Ralph. The purpose of my participation is spiritual, I remind myself. My own enjoyment is secondary.

From past experience, I expect Ralph will arrive exhausted and sleep deprived. An incorrigible procrastinator, especially when it comes to travel, Ralph postpones deciding about going until the last minute, then madly scrambles to prepare, finding one long-neglected task after another that must be tackled as he packs a single carry-on bag. The final two or three days are a frenzy of activity, with no possibility of sleep, and he breathlessly takes his assigned seat with moments to spare.

When Ralph arrives in Portland, he hasn't slept in two days. Within an hour of entering my home, he has adjusted the miniblinds in three rooms to their optimal angle for ambient light and privacy. I offer him the vegetarian food I've cooked for him—gazpacho made with a dozen different vegetables, black beans with cumin, carrots and celery, jasmine rice, date-nut bars. He says his stomach feels queasy and asks for canned soup.

After eating, Ralph promptly goes to bed and sleeps for twenty hours straight.

During his long slumber, I silently invoke the *mudita* phrases I've learned:

May your happiness not diminish.

May you enjoy abundance and peace.

May your joy and good fortune not leave you.

The night before the eclipse, I barely sleep. My down sleeping bag provides little padding against the lumpy desert floor. I wish I could use a chamber pot inside the tent, instead of having to unzip the fly, find my way by flashlight to the port-o-let, and hope for the best inside the filthy, overfull privy. By the wee hours of the morning I begin to drift off, only to be roused by Ralph beginning his early morning trips to the john. By six, he's up for good, and I hope to catch an hour of sleep before 7 a.m., the wakeup time set by Ralph the night before. All is quiet in the neighborhood.

"Orion!" announces Ralph loudly, presumably to a neighbor.

"What?" a woman asks softly.

"The constellation. Orion. See it there?"

"Oh, right . . . Orion."

Excitement growing in his voice, Ralph explains the factors affecting visibility of constellations. I give up on getting that extra hour of sleep, but not on my desire to rebuke Ralph for its loss.

"No one else is talking loud the way you are," I admonish, as I emerge from the tent.

But I needn't have blamed Ralph for making noise, because about then the charter planes begin to arrive at the airport, landing loudly on the runway and reminding us of the privileged few who can afford to swoop in and out for the prime event.

After breakfast, we set our chairs in front of the tent, facing east. The weather is perfect, the sky clear, with excellent visibility except for a little smoke from nearby wildfires. The eclipse will begin exactly at 9:06 a.m., with two minutes of totality starting at 10:19.

The atmosphere in the campground becomes even more hushed, as thousands of campers focus their attention on the sun. In anticipation, people try out their protective glasses, experiment with camera settings, apply sunscreen, and chat with neighbors.

People have come from all parts of the country as well as several other countries: England, Japan, Australia, Brazil. There are eclipse chasers who travel from one locale to the next, making plans years in advance to be in the right place at the precise moment. Once you experience the ecstasy of this celestial miracle, we're told, you're hooked for life. There's no way to describe the experience, they say; you must live it yourself to know its wonders.

Eclipse chasing can even become an addiction—no expense too great, no distance an obstacle, no effort excessive to experience the next rapture. The diehards fall into two camps. The amateur astronomers with their fancy equipment approach the event like a scientific study. The spiritual seekers prepare mentally for a transcendent epiphany. Both types are recognizable in the crowd surrounding our campsite.

As nine o'clock approaches, the background murmur slowly rises. The excitement is palpable. When the first sliver of sun disappears behind the moon, a man cries out, "There, it begins!" Through the glasses, it looks like someone has taken a small bite out of the sun's northeast rim. Slowly, the light around us fades, the temperature drops, and people crane their necks in all directions to take in the spectacle.

A crescendo of cries draws attention behind us, where Mt. Jefferson is bathed in the golden light of a seemingly setting sun. The quality of the light is strange, dreamlike. The air envelops our skin in cool caresses. No one looks in any direction too long, our gaze shifting above, below, left, right. People speak intimately to others in their party, not to neighbors. Our differences forgotten, Ralph and I hug and cheer and take photos, desperately trying to take in as much as possible.

Amid whoops and shouts and exclamations of joy, the sun goes completely dark. It takes a few seconds for me to realize I should remove my glasses to witness the corona, the brilliant ring of light encircling the sun during the total eclipse. Glasses off, my heart beats wildly as I witness the most dazzling sight of my life. The white-hot ring is stunning, the intensity of the light extraordinary. Witnessing it feels like a psychic cataclysm. I now understand what all the hoopla is about.

Near darkness surrounds the campground. I take a few steps in different directions. My gaze keeps returning to the incandescent circle in the sky. Time feels suspended. People around me seem to move in slow motion, their cries muffled through the electrified circuits of my mind.

Having missed the diamond-ring effect right before totality, I make sure to catch it on the other end. This is the brilliant starburst that appears briefly as the sun's rays shine over and under mountains and valleys on the moon's outer edge. The radiance is spectacular.

Then it's over. Too soon. Two minutes and 3.5 seconds of darkness.

Almost immediately, people around us begin to pack up and leave. But the eclipse isn't over yet. It will take the moon more than an hour to complete its passage across the sun.

We stay put. The chartered planes begin to fly out, and a long line of cars forms to exit the field. It will take over five hours to empty the campground. Someone said there were 9600 campers in our field alone, with several other campgrounds of similar size in the vicinity. Not in a hurry to get anywhere, we wait it out.

A few families are staying the night. One couple near our spot offer us to sit under their canopy while they explore a neighboring campground reported to offer music, food, and drinks.

The respite from the midday sun allows our sweltering bodies to cool. Ralph becomes engrossed in reading and responding to text messages. I bring out snacks. When he looks up, I offer him some. He declines and returns to texting. After a while, I take out my book and settle into reading. Just as I become engrossed in the story, Ralph tries to start a conversation about other celestial events of his life. I don't look up.

"What are you reading?" Ralph asks.

Accepting my fate, I reply, "It's a collection of essays by Ann Patchett. I'm reading the chapter about her approach to writing." I hope there might be pearls of wisdom awaiting my discovery on this momentous day.

After a brief pause, I return to reading.

Later, munching on a date-nut bar, Ralph asks if I baked the cookies myself. "Yes," I reply, grateful my culinary efforts are finally getting noticed. "I spent hours cooking for you."

"You needn't have," Ralph quips complacently. "I'm a man of simple needs." To prove his point, he eats an apple and some nuts, then declares, "See, fruit and nuts. That's my lunch."

When the couple with the canopy return, we crowd under a postage-stamp rectangle of shade and swap stories. We'd heard rumors that Elon Musk, Jeff Bezos and Phil Knight had camped at the airport. They share the scoop about a back way out of the field.

The exodus line thins as the sun sinks lower in the sky. Time to pack up and hit the road.

Anticipating that taking down the tent might strain our ability to work together, I suggest Ralph find places in the car to put away the chairs, cooler, and stove. That would give me time to roll up the sleeping bags and mats inside the tent. While I packed these items, Ralph could take down the tent.

Ralph's packing takes on new proportions, because one thing leads to another, and like-sized objects must be grouped together and rearranged. By the time I emerge from the tent, dripping sweat, the entire contents of the car are being reconfigured. I wipe my brow and begin pulling up stakes.

Just as I finish up with the tent, Ralph comes around the car holding an object in his open palm. It's one of two flashlights I packed for the trip.

"This," he says, with the solemnity of a headmaster scolding an errant pupil, "does *not* belong in the food basket. It was accidentally turned on, and the batteries would have burned out. Flashlights should be kept in a more accessible place. Put this in your purse or somewhere easy to get to."

"Oh my goodness," I exclaim. "How terrible! Just think—the batteries might have *burnt out*, and we have only *two sets* of replacements. By all means, let's store this properly," I say, taking the flashlight from him.

Ralph remains quiet as we finish packing the car.

We stay in Prineville over the next few days, visiting the Painted Hills, Smith Rock, and some other sites I'd recently explored on my vacation. Having a companion makes the second visit more interesting. I cringe when Ralph calls the motel housekeeping to complain about the absence of a light fixture over the bathroom sink.

In the car, Ralph's habit of humming becomes more pronounced, a soundtrack to our travels that registers his mood throughout the day. Mostly a steady, low hum which seems to signal relaxation, the sound shifts to a high-pitched keen in moments of concern. I feel grateful that I have no desire to comment on the humming.

I silently repeat again and again:

May your happiness and good fortune continue and increase.

Ralph looks back proudly on our eclipse experience as something he made happen. "I take credit for us having had this exciting adventure," he boasts on the way home. He's right, but my role went beyond logistical. It's enough that I know this. Unrecognized sympathetic joy still nourishes the soul.

Ralph never thanks me for changing my plans to enable him to experience the maximum eclipse. It never occurs to him I might have opted to stick with one minute in McMinnville. All I needed, he assumes, is time to come to my senses about a golden opportunity. Once, he offhandedly mentions I'd done a lot of preparation, but in my recollection, he never directly expresses appreciation for my efforts. In *his* memory, he later wrote, he had.

In hindsight, I see the flaw in my *mudita* practice. Sympathetic joy can't be tied to creating the conditions for another's happiness, especially at the expense of one's own.

Since his visit, Ralph and I have communicated little, and only by email. I sense a sea change in our relationship. In the end, the price paid for two minutes of totality might include a different kind of eclipse—that of a long-term friendship.

Building Community

To gain happiness and a sense of belonging in Portland, I needed to find a community of like-minded folks I could call "my people." With all the different groups I joined, I hoped one would emerge as my primary community, where I would make friends and socialize outside of organized events. At first I expected this bonding might occur in one of my volunteer settings or within Oregon Touch. When that didn't happen after two years, I organized my own groups and hosted gatherings to foster relationship building. I invested a great deal of effort in bringing together small clusters of friends and nurturing the groups so they would "gel" and become sustainable. These endeavors had mixed success, in large part because the social landscape of Portland is already saturated with competing opportunities.

One complaint you never hear in Portland is, "There's nothing to do around here." Instead, you might encounter, "Rats! My two favorite bands are playing the same night as the World Naked Bike Ride, and Gloria is hosting a planning session for next month's Tents for the Homeless project. What shall I do?" I encountered social butterflies who carried a list of ten events happening the same night and made short appearances at most of them.

The Rose City is flooded with social activities year-round, but particularly in summer the competition becomes so fierce, ongoing groups go on hiatus. Logistically, starting a new group amid so many events vying for people's time posed an enormous challenge. I reminded myself of this as I nurtured the groups I tried to establish, but I couldn't help feeling disappointment when the groups didn't thrive. I needed a peer support group badly.

My generation, boomers, saw the rise of support groups for every affliction, social identity, and life challenge on the planet. I spent the last two decades of my scholarly work studying illness support groups (breast cancer in Florida, elephantiasis in Haiti), especially the factors that predict group longevity. One important ingredient was the commitment of a critical mass of members to attend regularly in order to establish a core group that forms bonds of friendship and defines the norms and expectations for the group—the group's culture. The groups I organized in Portland lacked either a critical mass or shared expectations.

The Writing Group

The first group I put together was a writing critique group, in 2014. I had just completed a course in "The Art of the Personal Essay" from Portland Community College, and two classmates and I comprised the nucleus of our group. I invited three people to join whom I'd met in other contexts and who had expressed an interest in writing. The six of us met every other week to critique five-page submissions. Most members did no writing between meetings; they waited until the last minute then hastily wrote something to meet the deadline.

I was the only person in the group actively trying to publish my work. Others wrote for enjoyment or self-expression, with only vague plans for seeking a wider audience sometime in the future. One member consistently submitted excerpts from the autobiography he'd been writing for over two decades. The complete work comprised twenty-four volumes and over two million words. He rejected our advice to break up paragraphs spanning multiple pages, and he saw no problem with 125-word sentences. He confidently expected to find a publisher for his opus. Another member wrestled with a memoir ten years in the making that she couldn't finish. It wasn't unusual for people in this group to rebuff conventional writing wisdom with declarations like, "Please don't bring up those petty 'rules.' I have to write in my own authentic style."

After two years, my frustration with the group

came to a head. I'd hoped at least one person in the group would get serious about publishing so we could share experiences and I wouldn't feel like such an oddball. I proposed we adopt the expectation that at least once a year, each member would work on something for publication. My proposal was roundly rejected. To blatantly overgeneralize, Portlanders resist any outside pressure that constrains their unfettered self-expression. With regret, I left the writing group. After a few months, the autobiographer and the memoirist dropped out, and within a year the group had dissolved.

I wrote to my PCC writing teacher and asked about critique groups in Portland (the exclusive ones, the good ones, the ones he belonged to), but he replied that all the groups he knew of were closed.

Determined to find like-minded writers, I joined a Write to Publish Meetup that met across the river in Vancouver, Washington. There I found serious writers open to critical feedback and focused on getting published. Hallelujah! We met in a private room above a Thai restaurant. Reviewers skewered my academic sentence construction, reliance on the passive voice, and overuse of the word *that*. We had an "It Jar" in the center of the table, where each time someone used the word "it" in a piece, they had to deposit a quarter. Writers were not allowed to explain or dispute criticism. The sessions were long and sometimes ego-bruising, but everyone agreed the feedback improved their writing.

Sparsha: A Cuddly Women's Support Group

The next group I organized was described as a "cuddly women's support group." In truth, all I wanted was a women's group to talk about our lives, but I added the cuddly part because I wanted to invite people from Oregon Touch. I was just getting into Buddhism and decided to name the group *Sparsha*, Sanskrit for "touch." The group met a few times in my snuggle den upstairs, but only two or three people came besides me, and different ones each time. The group faltered and died.

For a while, I'd hoped the Oregon Touch group might become my community, but I didn't have much in common with the people I met there. Few people over sixty found their way to snuggle parties, so I always felt a bit out of place. Moreover, most of the snugglers, in addition to being polyamorous participants in sex positive groups, were involved in New Age subcultures such as ecstatic dance, Reiki, tantric yoga, alternative healing, and the study of chakras. I am not much of a New Age person. I even looked askance at the crystals lining the windowsill at my massage therapist's studio. And when it comes to relationships, I'm monogamous. The touch group was great for snuggling, but not a place for me to find community.

Spiritual Friends Group

After a near nervous breakdown precipitated by chicken raising in 2015, I began mindfulness meditation in earnest. I joined the Portland Insight Meditation Community (PIMC), took classes, and attended retreats. While perusing the center's website in search of community-building opportunities, I discovered spiritual friendship groups, known as Kalyana Mitta groups, gatherings of about a dozen people who met regularly for meditation and discussion of Buddhist precepts, or dharma. KM groups sounded like just what I needed. I contacted the coordinator and learned that the group meeting in southeast Portland was full and closed to new members, but perhaps I might be interested in forming a second group? I was!

We advertised the new group in July 2016 and began meeting in August. Following the guidelines for KM groups developed at Spirit Rock Meditation Center in California, we met for ninety minutes every other week, beginning with a check-in where people could share what's going on in their lives. We meditated for half an hour, took a break, and listened to a recording or read texts imparting a dharma lesson. Then we opened the floor for discussion and ended the meeting with a closing circle.

A guiding principle of KM groups is that cross talk is not allowed. When someone shares a personal story, expresses distress, or comments on the lesson, others should refrain from responding to what the person has said. Participants may comment on their own experience and ideas, but not give advice or express opinions about others' statements. I wholeheartedly embraced this rule, because one of the most challenging norms of American discourse is the tendency to approach every interaction as a problem-solving encounter. Also, being on the autism spectrum, I often struggled to find space in group conversation to interject what I wanted to say. Mindful listening without judgement or reaction, the heart of KM groups, doesn't come easily for most people. The no-cross-talk rule posed a challenge for our group as well, because the women continually pushed the boundaries toward an open exchange without constraints. Some members said they wished the group wasn't so "formal" and we could talk freely.

When I accepted the role of host and facilitator of the new group, I visited a couple of the other KM groups in town and got a sense of how they operated. All met in the same location each time, but responsibility for selecting the dharma content and moderating the meeting rotated among members. I expected our group to follow similar practices.

Only a few people came to the first few meetings, and many didn't return a second time. I had committed to keep the group going for at least three months, which would bring us to the holidays, when we'd reassess our prospects. By early December, of the ten people who'd contacted me about the group, all were women. It occurred to me we could make our group for women only, something I'd read about on the Spirit Rock website. When I proposed the idea, everyone agreed, and we became a women's group.

The main problem we faced was achieving a core membership who attended consistently. Typically, we had between three and six people at a meeting, at least one of whom was a new member who had to be introduced and oriented to our practices. It felt like the group had a rotating door on membership, with one or two old faces absent, and one or two new faces present each time. After three months, we hadn't reached a critical mass, and the members asked me to make a big recruitment effort—announcements at Sunday services and notices on the listserv.

Already feeling burned out over the failed touch groups, having to "beat the bushes" to get the group going discouraged me. Moreover, none of the women thus far had been willing to help out, so I was doing everything: communicating with members, hosting meetings at my home, preparing the content, and leading the meetings. More than I had bargained for!

After a recruitment push in January 2017, a new member, Alice, took an interest in selecting content, and eventually she became my cofacilitator for the group. Having a helper and feeling like I wasn't alone in the effort enabled me to stick with the group through the first few months of the year. But we still had turnover and inconsistent attendance. By April, I wanted out, but Alice encouraged me to give it one more try with new policies in place. We would implement the attendance policy recommended by Spirit Rock that asked newcomers to commit to attend every meeting possible for at least three months. At the end of the three-month period, if we hadn't achieved a core membership, we'd disband the group.

Alice and I explained this plan at our next meeting, noting the group had struggled to achieve consistent attendance since the beginning. Everyone agreed to abide by the new policy. But later a member privately expressed dissatisfaction with our attempt to "shame" people into going to meetings. We should just offer a good program, she advised, and if people liked it, they'd come back.

But I didn't get into this to "offer a program," I thought. *I just wanted a friendship group.*

After implementing the attendance policy, our group achieved a critical mass of six members and met regularly between April and July. Instead of feeling encouraged by this success, I felt burned out beyond recovery. A hurtful upbraiding from yet another member, this one offended by my announcement at a KM meeting about a women's snuggle party, felt like salt rubbed into a wound. Moreover, I realized that not everyone in Portland viewed peer cuddling as mainstream.

How had a simple quest to find community among friends led to a year-long strain ending in disappointment?

Our group came to a close after one year. Looking back on our experience, the biggest challenge seemed to be the constraints on interaction within KM groups that made it difficult to get to know people and develop true friendships. Yet the other KM groups in Portland, following the same norms, had succeeded. Did friendship ties already exist in those groups? Was our group's women-only composition a factor in its story? Surely my flawed leadership played a role.

Co-counseling Through Allies: People to People

The final community I auditioned to find my people was called Allies: People to People. This group broke away from its parent organization, Re-evaluation Counseling (RC), in the 1990s. I'd gotten into RC in the 1980s while living in Galveston, Texas. A colleague introduced me to the peer counseling system which had roots Scientology. The core practice is co-counseling, where two people take turns as the client and the counselor. What attracted me to the practice was its focus on "discharging" painful emotions like anger, fear, and frustration. My colleague and I enjoyed many counseling sessions where we shouted, wept, punched pillows, shook, laughed, and yawned. Despite its benefits, however, I dropped out of RC when I learned its tenets considered homosexuality abnormal and something to "work on" in counseling.

The Portland offshoot of RC rejected the offensive position on gays, changed the group's name, and attracted a large following of peer counselors. I first heard about the group while attending a retreat at the Great Vow Zen Monastery in Clatskanie, Oregon. The woman sitting next to me had been a long-term member of Allies, and she'd led their Raised Female Support Group. *Hey*, I thought, *this might be the answer to my prayers.*

With my curiosity peaked about how RC had survived a mutiny in Portland, I attended a ten-week orientation for Allies and refreshed my counseling skills. Afterwards, I tried a few sessions but realized the co-counseling approach to managing one's emotions was directly at odds with mindfulness meditation. In Buddhist philosophy, one should not indulge painful emotions and engage in venting. That only stirs up the emotion and makes it worse. One should calmly observe the feeling, accept it, and allow it to dissipate.

Which approach should I take? Acceptance or discharge? Detached observation or reliving the past? . . . I chose meditation. And gave up on finding community in Allies.

What did I have left? I attended Thursday night meditation and dharma talks at PIMC, which helped to steer me toward the right path. I was beginning to feel a part of that group, but the format wasn't conducive to making friends. The interpersonal exchanges there always seemed to occur in metta-speak, the hushed tones of someone quoting Buddhist scripture, unlike ordinary conversation where you got to know someone. Perhaps if I had joined the sangha sooner, I would have felt a greater sense of belonging.

After five years and exhaustive efforts to build community, I felt like a rootless plant, unable to find the right soil in which to thrive. But did my Portland experience differ much from my previous efforts to belong in the world as a normal person? I'd divorced when my children were young, struggled to find friendships and romantic partners, and maintained few collegial connections after leaving academia. The same loneliness and social isolation I'd experienced most of my life recurred in Portland. Yearning to understand my life, I wrote "Somewhere on the Spectrum," an account of my discovery, a decade earlier, a piece of the puzzle to my social failures. I believe that story holds a key to my inability to find home in Portland.

BUILDING COMMUNITY

ROSE CITY AUDITION

Somewhere on the Spectrum

When I was a teenager, my mother told me her doctor expected me to be born "blind and retarded." She only mentioned it once, her voice low and taut. My father never spoke of it at all. Why I never asked more questions about this prenatal event, I'm not sure, other than the realization at some deep level that the subject was taboo.

Sometime in her pregnancy my mother had caught rubella, or German measles as she called it. Dr. Carl, our family doctor, thought it best to shield her from the truth, saying nothing about risks to the baby. Instead, he told my father everything and instructed him to keep quiet about it until after the baby was born.

Inexplicably, from my mother's point of view, my father began going to Mass every day at 5 a.m. before leaving for work. At the same time, he stopped paying attention to the pregnancy and seemed indifferent to the growing baby. My mother felt emotionally abandoned and deeply hurt.

"Well, if you're not interested in this baby," she told him, "it's a bit late to figure it out."

Still, he kept his terrible secret.

After I was born, apparently normal, Dr. Carl and my Dad told my mother what had been going on. She didn't say how she felt about being kept in the dark, but the fact that this experience was mentioned only once in a lifetime speaks volumes.

I, too, treated the subject like a closed book until I turned fifty-five. Then, continuing my lifelong search for what was wrong with me, I returned to the gestation story, at first considering possible emotional damage based on failure to bond. As I mulled this over, a vague recollection surfaced about a link between congenital rubella and autism. I felt an instant rush that just possibly I had hit upon *the* burning question: Could my problem be that I was autistic?

I had many signs of the disorder: difficulty getting along with others; direct, blunt communication; heightened sensitivity to sensory stimulation; quick temper; literal thinking; difficulty recognizing faces; and a need for structure and rules.

My kindergarten teacher was my paternal grandmother, and she used to laughingly tell me how I often flew into rages in the classroom, screaming and pulling my pigtails straight out from my head.

As I gathered information on congenital rubella syndrome (CRS), I found two physical traits I had that also fit the profile of CRS: a heart murmur and a defect in one eye. Additional traits seemed to fit Asperger's disorder, or high-functioning autism. I took an online, self-administered test called the Asperger's Quotient,[6] developed by Simon Baron-Cohen at the Autism Research Centre in Cambridge, England, and scored in the range for Asperger's, according to the chart. One question in particular grabbed my attention. It asked the test taker if, when reading a story, he or she had difficulty imagining what a character looks like. I gasped when I read this. All my life I've found it impossible to visualize a fictional character's face, even when it is described in detail. In every book I've read, the characters all have blank faces.

But what really hit home for me emotionally was reading over and over how people on the autism spectrum suffer from loneliness and social isolation. *Loneliness and social isolation.* "That's me," I thought.

All of the scientific research on congenital rubella and autism was a few decades old at the time I started looking into it because the introduction of a universal vaccination for rubella in the 1970s eliminated most cases in the United States. After the MMR (measles, mumps, and rubella) vaccine became widely available, there were too few cases of the disease to conduct large-scale studies. However, in 1971 Stella Chess published an important study on autism in children exposed to rubella in utero[7] and a follow-up report in 1977.[8] What struck me about Chess's findings was the atypical nature of the autism cases tied to rubella.

The children in her study conformed to some of the features of classic autism, but not others. Later, when I was diagnosed as an "atypical" case, I would return to Chess's articles and carefully read every word.

The problem with being atypical is that most people don't believe it when I disclose my condition. They see me as a competent, successful professional with, at worst, a flawed personality, not someone with a disability. They experience my bluntness as rude, my interaction with others as weird, and my seriousness as a downer. In response, I try my best to blend in and appear normal, give the socially approved responses, force myself to smile more, and appear upbeat.

Determined to find answers, I made an appointment with an autism clinic at the university where I held a faculty position in the Department of Community and Family Health. Located within a child development center, the clinic served mostly young school children, although I was assured that some adults found their way there as well. When I expressed concern about being recognized in the waiting room, Dr. Davis, the psychologist I was to meet, offered to let me in the back door. The clinic had made this accommodation for another patient, one of the local professional football players. With stealth and apprehension, I hastened into a consultation room outfitted with toys and various child-focused diagnostic tools.

Dr. Davis was a young, attractive woman whom I warmed to immediately. She put me at ease and asked what seemed like all the right questions about what brought me to her door.

"So, what do you do when you find yourself in a group where someone is doing all the talking and you can't find the space to speak up?" she probed.

"Well, after holding my tongue until I can't stand it anymore, I usually say something like, 'Look, you've been talking for a while now. Would you mind if I took a turn?'"

"And how do people react when you say that?"

"They get angry and defensive and say something nasty to me."

"Okay, what else gets on your nerves in conversation with others?"

"Oh, where to start—well, one thing that happens often is I'll be talking about some problem, just wanting to vent about it, and the other person feels compelled to suggest ways to solve the problem. It drives me nuts! I just want the person to listen sympathetically and validate how I'm feeling. Instead, I get 'Have you tried this, have you tried that?' It's so frustrating."

She delved into my relationships with family, children, friends, and colleagues. I told her my biggest problems were loneliness and feeling rejected by others.

Following the interview, Dr. Davis administered a structured test called the Autism Diagnostic Observation Schedule that included, among other things, two tasks requiring one to use imagination and creativity. In the first task, I was given a random set of objects (shoelace, paper clip, small block, and playing card) and asked to make up a story using the items. For the second task, Dr. Davis gave me a booklet with line drawings like in a comic strip, but without any words, and told me to figure out what was happening in the story. In both exercises, according to Dr. Davis, my performance was below expectations. I used the objects literally as they were in real life instead of in a creative way (e.g., pretending the block was a car) and took an unusually long time to figure out the picture story.

After the test, Dr. Davis explained that my case fit the profile of a BAP, or broad autism phenotype, a "shadow syndrome" of the full-blown version. My insight and communication skills were good, and I did not show the hallmarks of Asperger's: unusual sensory interests, compulsive behaviors, self-injurious behavior, or complex hand or finger mannerisms. I demonstrated autism spectrum qualities that caused distress, but at a sub-clinical level, according to the official diagnostic criteria of the *DSM-IV* (*Diagnostic and Statistical Manual of Mental Disorders*, fourth edition).

In her evaluation report, Dr. Davis wrote that although I did not meet the diagnostic criteria for Asperger's disorder, I demonstrated significant social difficulties and would benefit from reading books explaining what it is like to live with the condition. She said my case was atypical and recommended I read *Build Your Own Life: A Self-Help Guide for Individuals with Asperger's Syndrome*, by Wendy Lawson,[9] and *Pretending to Be Normal: Living with Asperger's Syndrome*,[10] by Liane Holliday Willey. She also recommended therapy with a professional familiar with high functioning autism/ Asperger's disorder and provided a referral.

Since my motivation for getting evaluated was to better understand myself (rather than to be approved for insurance coverage for therapy), the report didn't disappoint me. I welcomed the validation that my social impairment was serious and real. Finally, I had an explanation for my long struggle to relate to people and maintain good relationships. I spent hours mentally sifting through a lifetime of experiences and viewing them through the prism of autism. I recalled the time I asked one of the doctoral students in my program if she had any suggestions to help me get along better with students. "Look at the students when you talk to them," she replied without skipping a beat. Until that point, I was unaware I did not make enough eye contact. Since then I've trained myself to do it more. I remembered all the times my mother and others admonished me to smile more and talk more, to be less withdrawn. I reflected on the frequent aggravation I feel toward others who do not respond in the ways I want, and I considered my need to have certain conversational dynamics to feel at ease. I thought of all the friendships I'd lost from coming across as too confrontational and of my tendency to take things literally and not get jokes. I thought of how easily I experience sensory overload, especially from sound, and how I jump in fright when someone touches or speaks to me unexpectedly.

When I began to talk about this with family and friends, the reactions were mixed. Some people immediately recognized what I described and accepted my explanation, while others scoffed and said, "No way are you autistic." The naysayers insisted I was too regular and too successful career-wise to have such a problem and perhaps I was just mistaking being introverted for autism. I was grateful my children fell into the believer camp, citing examples of behavior they had observed that fit the pattern, like how quickly I became frustrated, and recalling awkward moments of social interaction they had witnessed. One son confided that, growing up, he often wished I would act more like other parents.

I began thinking of myself as being "somewhere on the spectrum" and read everything I could find online and in books and magazines. The volumes recommended by the psychologist were helpful, but the one that really spoke to me was *Women from Another Planet?: Our Lives in the Universe of Autism*,[11] by Jean Kearns Miller. A collaborative effort by a group of afflicted women, the book focuses on the special challenges faced by high-functioning women on the spectrum. One of the most common difficulties the women discussed was convincing people they had a real problem. So much of the effort to conform "does not show at all on the outside." They heard the usual retort—"Oh, I have that too sometimes"—when they mentioned an autism behavior or characteristic, such as "wanting to be alone too much," being "deliberately rude and unfriendly," or the disruption felt when even inviting a friend over could seem like "having a strange person in the house."

In the Miller book, Wendy talked about having "to put on a personality" she had constructed, "as though rehearsing for a play, then getting up on stage." Gail noted how she hated to talk to people "who do this phony baloney stuff well. All this false politeness and good will." She felt like "smacking them and saying, 'Tell me what you are really thinking!'" Ava, on the other hand, highlighted the curious mix of "ability and disability, success and failure, insight and naiveté" found among high-functioning persons. I identified strongly with Jane's observation that she was "much more isolated than those around [her] ever suspect." And finally, a stanza from Susan's poem hit home:

> Among the words
> I most dread to hear,
> Yet hear so often,

Are "Lighten up!"
"Don't be so intense."
"Don't take life so seriously."
In essence you are telling me
To stop functioning.

From the Miller book and other sources, I learned about the "neurodiversity" movement, which promotes greater acceptance of people who think and act differently from the "neurotypical" norm, the idea being that *society* needs to change to accommodate those with psychological differences, not the reverse. Also, taking a cue from the disability movement, "autistic culture" views autism as a set of values, beliefs, and behavior; people on the spectrum can feel part of and make positive contributions to that culture. With my anthropological background, the idea of a shared culture as a source of pride appealed to me.

I even twice attended Autreat, an annual gathering of autistic persons in Pennsylvania with the stated purpose of focusing on "positive living with autism, NOT on causes, cures, or ways to make us more normal." There, for the first time, I felt no pressure to maintain a pleasant smile and cheery demeanor. I could go around with a blank expression on my face, and no one seemed to take notice. Attendees wear name tags identifying their preference for being approached and spoken to or for being left alone. It's considered perfectly normal to sit alone in the cafeteria and show no interest whatsoever in meeting other people. For me the experience was deliciously liberating and strengthened my identity as an Aspie.

In 2013, the *DSM-V* eliminated the diagnosis of Asperger's disorder, moving it into the general category of autism spectrum disorder, now differentiated by *level* of impairment. A few of my skeptical friends cited this as further evidence I did not have a real condition. I viewed the change as a step in the right direction, placing emphasis on degree of impairment instead of on meeting a unique set of criteria. I wondered how my clinical evaluation would have differed under the new guidelines.

Ten years after gaining insight into my "problem," hardly a day goes by that I don't think about some new happenstance that makes the most sense within the framework of autism. Having this mind-set is a mixed blessing. The insights are healing, but being afflicted with just a "touch of autism" is frustrating because so many of its effects remain invisible to others. They can't see the strain behind holding a simple conversation, having to be ever vigilant about saying the wrong thing or coming across as "strange." They are unaware of the mental effort to remember to smile and appear animated. Nor do they realize how much is held back, unsaid, or that my offensive remarks don't represent uncensored, unrestrained outspokenness. Still, others accept that I have this condition, but they nevertheless get tired of having to accommodate my needs.

While I would not describe myself as a militant for neurodiversity, I have adopted the ideology and values associated with the movement. I believe we should promote greater social acceptance of people on the spectrum. It also occurred to me that as I get older, it seems harder to force myself to conform to neurotypical expectations. I am increasingly inclined to explain my needs and hope people will be sympathetic and accommodating. As when I first "came out," the reactions to these overtures have been mixed. I am fine with that. As long as a few close family and friends continue to support me, I am grateful.

When I moved to Portland, I made an extra effort to fit in, come across as normal, and censor my tendencies to appear confrontational. With people I hoped to become friends, I explained how my direct style of communication and need for certain conversational dynamics might rub them the wrong way at times, and I asked for their understanding. These disclosures seemed to help people understand me, but I'm not sure that led to greater acceptance. The people I met already had satisfying social networks and seemed disinclined to accommodate someone outside the norm.

The greatest benefit I gained from the Portland experience in terms of my autism was learning through insight meditation how to practice loving kindness toward myself and to find deeper acceptance of my ongoing struggles. I began to recognize the ways in which I compounded the problem by wanting things to be different than they were, then feeling disappointed when they weren't. Acceptance of things the way they are is the core lesson I took with me.

ROSE CITY AUDITION

Finding Home

In how many ways can one fail and still say,
Hey, I did it!

On the fifth anniversary of my arrival in Portland, October 2, 2017, I reflected on my sojourn thus far. My son, Elliot, had left Seattle in February and moved back to Tampa to be near friends. I missed our bimonthly visits. About once a month I attended a snuggle party sponsored by Daniella, a wise, loving person who began offering platonic events after I left Oregon Touch. I belonged to a sangha and felt part of a global Buddhist community. I'd completed a certificate in editing from UC Berkeley Extension in July and hoped to develop a freelance editing business. I'd experienced a total solar eclipse and survived a rocky friendship to tell the story. Now, I began planning another big geographic move. This time, I'd go full circle, back to Louisiana, where I grew up and hadn't lived for forty-five years.

Given how hard I'd worked to become a Portlander, how could I give up living in the Promised Land, only to rejoin the ranks of the silent minority in a scarlet state? Where it's hot and humid and infested with mosquitoes. Where a law was passed with the specific intent of stating the punishment for stealing crawfish. But, hopefully, where most people wouldn't have a problem with the French pronunciation of Jeannine.

By July 2016, I'd made the decision to move, but at a future date, after I'd experienced everything I could in Portland. In Louisiana, I would live near my five brothers and their wives, fifteen nieces and nephews, fourteen grand-nieces and nephews, and a slew of cousins. There would always be a birthday party, wedding, or graduation ceremony to attend if I wanted to spend time with loved ones. The timeline for the move accelerated after my ill-timed bunionectomy in January 2017, which left me fearful of getting sick and having no one to look after me. It became clear I needed family members I could count on to have my back in a crisis.

My podiatrist, Dr. Ling, had cautioned me about the "social debt" incurred by foot surgery, the price tag for enlisting help from one's social network. The term he used intrigued me—and instilled apprehension—because I wasn't confident I had enough social capital in Portland to get the help I needed in the first place, much less incur debt.

That the surgery was planned for Friday, the 13th of January might have foreshadowed the bad luck to come. The following Monday I had a follow-up appointment scheduled to check for swelling and complications. I needed transportation to and from the hospital on Friday, someone to help out the first three days, and rides to and from the follow-up visit. To cover all this assistance, I enlisted five friends and my son Elliot, who would come from Seattle for the weekend. My friend Martha would stay with me after the surgery until Elliot arrived. All seemed set until Portland was blanketed with the worst snow and ice storm in decades. The entire city ground to a halt.

Portland doesn't get much snow, only about three inches per year. When it does, the snow usually melts quickly and the roads clear within a couple of days. During the storm, I read withering accounts of the city's snow policy: Wait till it melts. Consequently, the city doesn't own much equipment to clear away snow and ice. Moreover, the city had banned the use of rock salt to melt roadway ice, and the green alternatives were less effective.

Two days before my surgery, twelve inches of snow fell in Portland, followed by freezing rain. The temperature hovered below freezing for over a week. Portland was paralyzed. The mayor declared a state of emergency. All but the main roads were impassable without snow tires or chains. Schools and businesses closed. People couldn't even move their cars out of their driveways, much less drive on treacherous streets. Hospitals, however, were prepared to operate in all weather, so my surgery wasn't canceled.

Everyone I had lined up to help, except Elliot, called to cancel. Even Martha, who doesn't own a car and planned to take the bus, bowed out because just walking to the bus stop posed danger. One of my five friends had tire chains in her garage, but she didn't feel confident enough to put them on. I called five more people from my address book, but none could help. I contacted Visiting Angels, the Oregon Department of Elder Affairs, and Easter Seals (someone suggested them). No transportation or other services were available on a one-time basis. Only enrolled clients qualified for assistance. I didn't feel secure calling a taxi or Uber because I'd need assistance negotiating the front steps and slick driveway. Besides, I wasn't sure if hospital policy would allow me to return home with a stranger. When I had a colonoscopy at the same place, the rules required that a family member or friend drive me home.

I scrambled at the last minute to find a ride to the hospital with one of my neighbors who had a four-wheel drive. Thank God Elliot was able to come and help over the weekend, but I still needed support after that and had no one to call. I had trouble getting around the house, fixing food, and taking a shower. I cried a few times.

Finding transportation to the follow-up appointment was traumatic. I canceled the Monday appointment for lack of a ride and rescheduled for Tuesday not knowing how I'd get there. Having exhausted my list of friends, in desperation I searched the website of the Portland Insight Meditation Center, where I studied Buddhism, for something like a Care Committee. They had one! When I received an email reply from the contact person, she said their committee hadn't been active for a long time and should be removed from the website, but she would try her best to find someone to take me.

A guy named Mike, whom I'd never met, kindly agreed to give me a ride. We worked out a plan and exchanged phone numbers. When he hadn't arrived by fifteen minutes after the pickup time, I called his cell phone and got voicemail. Panic. Was he stuck somewhere without phone service? Should I call the doctor's office to cancel again? But I didn't want to cancel because what if my foot was swelling inside the cast, or bleeding internally, or . . . .

A scruffy-looking man with longish grey hair arrived in an old van half an hour late. Following introductions, I asked Mike, "Did you get my voicemail?" He answered no, checked his phone log, and said he'd ignored my call because the number had an out-of-state area code.

"I was worried you weren't coming," I said anxiously, "because I assumed you'd call to let me know if you'd be late."

"Now, maybe I wasn't the right person to do this if it's something where you have to be there at an exact time. It's taken me an hour driving over ice just to get here," he said, sounding aggrieved.

Suddenly, I felt in danger. I had pissed off this man and had no idea how to make nice to him. I found myself dependent on a total stranger to get me to a doctor's appointment to find out if my foot was bleeding internally.

"I appreciate your help," I said contritely. Nerves on edge, I sat silently for the rest of the ride. At the clinic, Dr. Ling pronounced my foot in fine shape.

What shocked me most about the subsequent days of my recovery? None of the friends who'd been lined up to help me get through the surgery, nor any other Portland friend who knew about it, called to check on me, much less offer to help. It seemed I couldn't count on anyone to have my back, even in times of crisis. I felt alone and unprotected. My decision to move to Louisiana sooner rather than later solidified during that difficult period.

Like Fieldwork, Highs and Lows

The more I reflected on my sojourn, the more the experience reminded me of the highs and lows of cross-cultural fieldwork. I'd experienced the ups and downs of working in a foreign setting—Haiti, Rwanda, Uganda, Dominican Republic, Costa Rica,

France—and recalled similar feelings of elation and despondency, fascination and ennui, as I navigated unfamiliar territory. I remembered the miserable week I spent in Uganda, ravaged by dysentery, with only a stern, unsympathetic team leader to look in on me. But on that trip I saw the source of the Nile! In Haiti, I suffered from dengue fever and wrestled with maddening logistics, but at the same time enjoyed decades of gratifying work. My relationship with Portland felt like studying another culture, relishing the highs, but consigned to accept the lows.

The Highs

Topping the list of high points in my Portland experience, I cherished living in a community that takes environmental protection seriously. Where receptacles for waste recycling are provided at every public event. Where protesters suspended from the St. Johns Bridge successfully thwarted an icebreaker ship headed to drill for Alaskan oil. Where people brag at parties about how many bicycle miles they commuted or how few miles they drove in the previous year. Where you see bumper stickers that read, "Trees Are the Answer."

In Portland, for the first time in my life, I was surrounded by progressive-minded people who cheered in public for liberal causes. I got to visit the majestic natural wonders of Oregon. My fantasies about finding nurturing touch among peers were realized through wonderful snuggle parties. At these events, I got to know transgender persons as real people. Being able to walk to shops selling legal cannabis in herbal and edible variety never ceased to amaze me. I reveled in watching new-release films in single-screen movie theaters with five-buck admission.

I appreciated being able to hop on a bus or light rail to go anywhere in the metro area, having access to bicycle lanes and thruways, and observing the respect shown to pedestrians.

My preference for a natural look fit well in Portland. Body hair on women is normal and doesn't attract attention. I could go most places without makeup and not feel self-conscious. Long grey hair on women was commonplace.

The Lows

The flip side of a city being a desirable place to live, with heavy in-migration, is the pejorative image of transplants. Speaking about the problem of burgeoning traffic congestion, a meditation teacher joked, "All of you who moved here in the past five years, go home." Long-term residents looked upon recent arrivals (i.e., within the past ten years) as interlopers. I attended an event early on where people took turns introducing themselves and saying how long they'd lived in Portland. When I said, "Six weeks," everyone laughed and said, "You really are a newbie!" Years later, at a garden party, I proudly stated I had lived in Portland four years. "Oh, so you're still a newbie, then," my listener replied. I realized I would never escape the transplant identity. The audition to become a real Portlander would continue without end.

Although by no means unique to Portland, the city's housing problems detracted from its ambience: demolition of older homes to build apartment complexes or luxury homes; rent escalation and diminishing affordable housing; gentrification and displacement; blight and suffering from homelessness. And yes, relentless overcast, misty weather really sucks, especially after living in the Sunshine State for a quarter century. At the same time, I had to laugh at weather reports of precipitation measured in hundredths of an inch. I missed real thunderstorms!

My fear of earthquakes was real. I experienced a minor one while sitting at my desk on the second floor of my first apartment, just a few months after arriving in Portland. The evening news reported the quake's magnitude as only 2.5, but I'd definitely felt the building sway from side to side for seconds in a way that elicited a disturbing sense of floating on air. I'll take hurricanes before earthquakes any day; at least you can evacuate in time for a storm.

In the US Southeast, I'd experienced no shortage of nuisance insects—roaches, flies, mosquitos, you name it. But Portland propagated an exceptionally odious species of large black flies that seemed to appear out of nowhere inside one's home, impossible to ambush or scare out the door. Their incessant acrobatics and loud buzzing drove me nuts.

Portland's bicycle and pedestrian friendly manners had a downside. One of my biggest fears was accidentally hitting a bicyclist with my car. As a pedestrian, I hesitated to stand too near a curb lest an oncoming vehicle screech to a stop.

I never accustomed to the exaggerated cheerfulness of help staff in stores, especially those in artisan boutiques and cannabis shops. Their over-the-top demeanor felt like pressure to match the person's annoying buoyancy.

Portlandia ruined satire about Portland for me. When I write outlandish things about the city, readers wonder if I'm describing something real or made up.

Having grown up in Louisiana, a state with the nickname Sportsman's Paradise, I enjoyed fishing and even joined the Fishing 101 Meetup. Yet I had to be careful about mentioning such controversial practices because some Portlanders considered the killing of other beings unethical. When I mentioned a fishing trip to one of my Buddhist buddies, she blanched and expressed sympathy for the fish. Moreover, for all the Northwest's appreciation of Dungeness crabs, locals eat them incredibly bland, and stores don't sell crab boil seasoning.

How the Deck Stacked

Five years in Portland had tarnished my idealized image of the ultimate progressive city. I still considered the city a model for healthy, sustainable community, but to achieve a sense of belonging posed challenges exceeding my resources. Life stage, temperament, social competence, singlehood, absence of family support, weak friendship bonds, misguided choices, all affected my experience.

Psychologist Tara Brach coined the term "severed belonging" to describe ruptures in our sense of connection to our social environment, the loss of feeling known and accepted by those around us. Such fissures often instill distorted beliefs that there is something wrong with us, which, in turn, can lead to loneliness and melancholy. Developing self-compassion through meditation can heal severed belonging, according to Brach. I believe this solace was the key draw of meditation for me.

Being single in a society organized around couples undoubtedly played a role in my Portland experience. I don't recall socializing with any couples, just the three of us. Once my male friends found girlfriends, they stopped spending time with me. Mostly I spent time with other single women near my age. I'm convinced that had I been part of a couple living on my block, we'd have been invited inside the home of at least one neighbor. Most likely, that would have been Jim and

Jenny a few doors down, who moved to Sellwood to be near their daughter and grandchildren. The three of us had friendly conversations on the sidewalk, but our talk conformed to the Portland Politesse variety.

Had I embarked on chicken raising with an adult partner, the burden of care could have been shared, and perhaps I would have coped better.

A guy in his forties I met at a snuggle party talked about the "stress of being single." The countless ways going through life alone exacts a cost. The strain is hidden and pernicious.

Where is Home?

Readers expecting to learn about an epiphany of insight, where I realized my true home is within myself, won't find it here. Since Buddhism teaches us to "Come home to ourselves," to look within for enlightenment, one might expect such a discovery as not only believable, but a culturally scripted resolution for my problem. That wasn't my experience. Meditation helped me calm incessant rumination, make fewer judgments, develop self-compassion, and accept things the way they are. But I still felt a yearning for intimate conversation with other people.

Sometime during 2017 I read a magazine article that quoted various experts on things we can do to stay healthy. A psychiatrist said the single thing we can do to protect our mental health is to spend at least ten minutes each day in conversation with a loved one. *Wouldn't that be wonderful*, I thought. Typically, I talked to my sons about once every other week, and perhaps to a brother or sister-in-law a few times a year. After Elliot moved, in-person conversation with loved ones happened about twice a year. Sometimes I looked forward to meeting with my therapist simply to talk intimately with a live person.

I had hoped one or two of my Portland friends might welcome me into the inner circle of their families, but that never happened, even when I voiced a desire to be included. They projected the attitude, "I am not my sister's keeper." After someone in my writing group read this essay, she commented, "We could all give more to people needing friendship." Her words warmed my heart. Mother Theresa got it right when she said, "The problem with the world is that we draw the circle of our family too small."

As I told someone during my last months in Portland, "It's not enough to live in a cool city. You need to be around loved ones."

I spent my last year in Portland seeing an excellent psychologist who helped me understand why I failed to develop a sense of belonging with the groups I tried and why I found only casual friends, not confidants. "You set your sights on becoming a Portlander and embracing everything special the city had to offer," she explained. "You selected groups based on your interests and those offering lifestyles not found in other places. To find 'your people,' you need to target groups where you'd likely find women like yourself—older, professional, civically engaged." She suggested I try organizations like the League of Women Voters. I promised to follow her advice once settled in Louisiana.

My sights are set on reconnecting with my family of origin. I have no idea how that will go. I will return as the prodigal daughter, the one who couldn't wait to escape the confines of a conservative community, only to return more than four decades later seeking its embrace. Returning to reclaim, if I am fortunate, a sense of belonging. A few of my old friends used the term "eating crow" when told of my planned return. Hopefully the ones I care about will welcome me back. My autistic challenges certainly will follow me back home, and I'll face the usual adjustment to a new community, but with any luck, one made easier through loving support.

A few weeks before the anniversary of my foot surgery, I accidentally yanked my fireplace door off its hinges and dropped it on my foot, the one not operated on, fracturing the little toe.

"So, I hear you injured your little toe. You needed to do something so you could come see me again, " joked Dr. Ling, my podiatrist.

Hardly, I thought. *You wouldn't be saying that if you knew how little social debt I incurred during the surgery last year*. But being the cooperative patient, I chuckled along and said, "That's right."

"Here's where your toe is fractured," said Dr. Ling, pointing to a spot on the x-ray that looked to me like a blur. He manipulated the toe and said, "Heard that click?"

I shivered at the thought of my bone clicking. The visit concluded without further instruction because nothing could be done for a broken toe except to take pills to control pain, which was minimal.

As he approached the door to leave, Dr. Ling turned to say, "You know, this is going to be a good year. Last year was a bad one, but this year will be different."

I knew he meant we would soon begin the Chinese New Year, the Year of the Dog, an auspicious symbol of good fortune. I hoped he was right.

As I exited the building, my spirits began to lift, and I noticed a spring in my limp.

Epilogue

A year has passed since my move back to Louisiana. There are many things I miss about Portland—urgent concern for the future of the planet and human rights, access to mass transit and nurturing touch, communitarian values—but I don't regret leaving. As I'd hoped, I feel a greater sense of belonging in the familiar environment of Cajun culture, the Louisiana landscape, and my family of origin. Yet the reality is that, once more, I'm a transplant, facing the inevitable adaptation and entrée into a new setting. I'm weathering the growing pains of putting down roots, but at least the soil is familiar, even if it isn't perfectly matched to my needs. It will take years to weave myself into the fabric of this new home. Daily I cultivate patience with the process. Often I remind myself to let go of expectations.

After months of weary house-hunting, I settled into a modest 1930s bungalow near downtown Lafayette. My new neighborhood occupies a transitional zone between a middle-class area with mostly white residents and the city's oldest, mostly black community. One block east of my house, a concrete-lined coulee marks the racial boundary. The city's residential segregation seems antiquated, but its ethnic diversity feels familiar to me. African Americans make up about one-third of the population, and Hispanics, Native Americans and Asians about ten percent. A few blocks away a soul food restaurant featured on Anthony Bourdain's *Parts Unknown* garnered praise for its popularity with a mixed clientele, but outside of food, music and a few churches, social circles don't seem to overlap much within the city.

Several neighbors have invited me into their homes to visit or share meals. This welcoming friendliness contrasts sharply with my experience in Portland. Indeed, people who've moved here from elsewhere often comment on the remarkable friendliness of folks in Acadiana. Having grown up in a small town nearby and attended the local university as an undergraduate helps my social acceptance. Being able to say "I'm from Ville Platte" grants me provisional entree into the fold. At the same time, having left for forty-five years and most recently lived on the oft-maligned West Coast raise suspicion that I might be tainted. I consciously find ways to validate my good ol' girl credentials when interacting with others.

Despite the friendliness, however, establishing close ties with people here seems just as hard as in

Portland. Family members, old friends, and new acquaintances all have full, busy lives and aren't looking to fill gaps in their social network, as I am. At my life stage most people are focused on their own multi-generational families and long-term friendships. As I anticipated, opportunities arise for family gatherings to celebrate life events and holidays, but more intimate interactions in smaller groups are hard to come by. So far, the onus rests with me to initiate such encounters, which is only fitting for the one who left. With time, I hope that changes.

While chicken raising constituted my nemesis in Portland, getting my Lafayette house into a livable condition dealt a traumatic blow. Major upgrades were needed just to get homeowners insurance, but rewiring the electrical system proved dreadful. Few electricians welcomed the onerous job of replacing knob and tube wiring. After being turned down repeatedly or told I'd have to wait weeks, I put my faith in Home Advisor's online matching service, which promised verification of credentials and background checks. Instead, I got an unqualified heroin addict with a homeless assistant who began sleeping in my guest room, wrapping himself in curtains to stay warm. The motley crew did abysmal work and violated city regulations, landing me in trouble with the authorities. Finding a reputable company to rescue the operation took effort, and I spent weeks lying awake at night, worried about ever escaping the mess. In the end I found someone for big bucks and vowed I'd never again undertake house renovation.

When I left Louisiana the movement to preserve the French language and culture had just launched. Over the decades, "Cajunization" had saturated the region with Acadian-themed business names and bilingual signage, but little French is spoken today. To my disappointment, few people can pronounce my name the francophone way. When someone does, I feel embraced.

Unlike in Portland where I vigorously sought new experiences, here I let things evolve organically. My meditation practice helps me accept things as they come. I've refrained from joining new organizations and instead focus on a quiet life of reflection, writing, gardening, and exploring the countryside.

Already I've gratefully relied on the support of family and friends to help me through a medical scare, this one following complications of cataract surgery which left me visually impaired and unable to drive for three months. I used the time confined to my home as a spiritual retreat, spending hours each day in meditation and listening to dharma talks. With good fortune, I found an insight meditation center in Lafayette where a small group meets regularly. My backyard will soon be transformed into a garden for peaceful contemplation.

EPILOGUE

The most significant dividend of my Portland sojourn was finding a spiritual compass that continues to transform my worldview. I embraced the Rose City wholeheartedly, savored its delights, then returned home to Louisiana without misgivings to chart a new path toward a meaningful life.

NOTES

1. Deborah Tannen, *You're the Only One I Can Tell: Inside the Language of Women's Friendships*, (New York: Ballantine, 2017), 238.

2. Dave Wheitner, *The Snuggle Party Guidebook: Create Deeper Friendships, Decrease Loneliness, & Enjoy Nurturing Touch Community*, Version 1.1, (Portland, OR: Divergent Drummer Publications, 2014), 145-47.

3. Alexander Barrett, *This Is Portland: The City You've Heard You Should Like*, (Portland, OR, Microcosm Publishing, 2013).

4. Robert Litt and Hannah Litt, *A Chicken in Every Yard: The Urban Farm Store's Guide to Chicken Keeping*, (Berkeley, CA: Ten Speed Press, 2011).

5. "Pointers for Novice and First-Time Rose Exhibitors," Portland Rose Society website, last accessed September 28, 2019, http://www.portlandrosesociety.citymax.com/f/Pointers_for_Showing_Roses.pdf.

6. "Autism Spectrum Quotient (AQ)," Autism Research Centre, University of Cambridge, last accessed September 28, 2019, https://www.autismresearchcentre.com/arc_tests.

7. Stella Chess, "Autism in Children Exposed to Rubella in Utero," *Journal of Autism and Childhood Schizophrenia* 1, no. 1 (1971):33-47.

8. Stella Chess, "Follow-Up Report on Autism in Congenital Rubella," *Journal of Autism and Developmental Disorders* 7, no. 1 (1977): 69–81.

9. Wendy Lawson, *Build Your Own Life: A Self-Help Guide for Individuals with Asperger's Syndrome*, (London: Jessica Kingsley, 2003).

10. Liane Holliday Willey, *Pretending To Be Normal: Living with Asperger's Syndrome*, (London: Jessica Kingsley, 1999).

11. Jean Kerns Miller, *Women from Another Planet?: Our Lives in the Universe of Autism*, (Bloomington, IN: AuthorHouse, 2003).

About the Author

M. J. Coreil is a cultural anthropologist turned essayist who uses personal experience and satire to shine light on social issues. Her creative writing has appeared in *PsychCentral, Huffington Post, the Satirist, Oregon Humanities*, and *Ursa Minor*. Some of her work can be found at tropicofcandor.com.

www.ingramcontent.com/pod-product-compliance
Lightning Source LLC
Chambersburg PA
CBHW021100080526
44587CB00010B/317